COURAGE   DETERMINATION

TEAMWORK   PERSISTENCE

INTEGRITY   CITIZENSHIP

JUSTICE   COMMITMENT

EXCELLENCE   **JACKIE'S NINE**

DETERMINATION   TEAMWORK

PERSISTENCE   INTEGRITY

CITIZENSHIP   JUSTICE

COMMITMENT   EXCELLENCE

EXCELLENCE   COURAGE

DETERMINATION   TEAMWORK

PERSISTENCE   INTEGRITY

COURAGE DETERMINATION TEAMWORK PERSISTENCE

JACKIE'S NINE

*Jackie Robinson's
Values to Live By*

INTEGRITY PERSISTENCE COMMITMENT EXCELLENCE

SHARON ROBINSON

Scholastic Inc. / New York

No part of this publication may be reproduced in whole or in part, or stored in a retrieval system, or transmitted in any form or by any means, electronic, mechanical, photocopying, recording, or otherwise, without written permission of the publisher. For information regarding permission, write to Scholastic Inc., Attention: Permissions Department, 555 Broadway, New York, NY 10012.

0-439-23764-5

Text copyright © 2001 by Sharon Robinson, unless otherwise noted on pages 177–178 All rights reserved. Published by Scholastic Inc. SCHOLASTIC and associated logos are trademarks and/or registered trademarks of Scholastic Inc.

Library of Congress Cataloging-in-Publication Data available
12 11 10 9 8 7 6 5 4 3 2 1   01 02 03 04 05

Book design by Elizabeth B. Parisi

Printed in the U.S.A.   23
First Scholastic printing, May 2001

To my parents, Rachel and Jack,
who taught me through their actions to love deeply,
give generously, and stay in the struggle.
— S.R.

TABLE OF CONTENTS

INTRODUCTION

I WAS SIX WHEN MY DAD RETIRED from Major League Baseball and twelve when he was elected into baseball's Hall of Fame. I was sixteen the first time my boyfriend hit me; eighteen when my brother Jackie was arrested for drug possession; and twenty when I took control of my life. When I was twenty-one, Jackie was killed in a car accident; my dad had a massive heart attack and died when I was twenty-two.

I'm no stranger to obstacles.

At eighteen, I was terrified of failure and measured success based on the model set by my celebrity parents. By twenty-three, I'd begun to measure success on my own terms. Since then, I've earned degrees at Howard and Columbia Universities, raised a wonderful son, published three books, and as a nurse–midwife, delivered close to 700 babies.

At age forty-seven, I retired from midwifery and joined the Office of the Commissioner of Baseball as Director of Educational Programming. I launched

Breaking Barriers: In Sports, In Life. This educational program uses baseball-themed activities as teaching tools and brings baseball players into classrooms across the country, where they talk about how they overcome obstacles on and off the field.

Breaking Barriers is based on the nine values that I associate with my father's life. Why nine, you might ask? Well, it's really quite simple. Within baseball, the number nine is a common denominator. There are nine innings, nine player positions, and the base path is ninety feet between each base. Therefore it was appropriate that there be nine values celebrated in both *Breaking Barriers* and in this book.

Which leads me into why I wrote *Jackie's Nine.* Well, part of it was that I wanted to build on the success of the *Breaking Barriers* program. I wanted to continue spreading the program's message about the importance and universality of my father's values. I also was motivated by a conversation I once had with Jesse Jackson.

In 1987, my son, Jesse, and I spent Thanksgiving with the Reverend Jackson and his family at their home in Chicago. After dinner, a few of us sat in the living room talking. Our conversation led to a discussion about my father. We talked about why some athletes' fame lives on and others' fades with time. The reason, Reverend Jackson explained, lay in the difference between a champion and a hero. A champion, he said, wins a World Series or an Olympic event and is hoisted on the shoulders of teammates and fans. A hero carries the people on his shoulders. Champions live for the moment — heroes, like Jackie Robinson, transcend time.

To help bring life to my father's legacy, each chapter in *Jackie's Nine* celebrates one of his values and includes a scene from my life and one from my dad's to help illustrate the principle. I've also chosen a selection in each chapter about the life of one of my heroes. This gave me an opportunity to pay tribute to courageous men and women who have touched me personally, though I found it very difficult to limit my choice to one individual per chapter.

Inspired by the high expectations and stellar examples of my heroes (and *she*roes), I strive for excellence as an educator, writer, and parent. Their courage makes me feel hopeful and gives me the strength to look for the new possibilities in life's challenges.

Whether you're playing a game of baseball or rounding the bases of life, we all need some structure to successfully make the journey. The principles in *Jackie's Nine,* beginning with courage and building toward excellence, provide a foundation. In between these two are chapters about the other values my dad lived by: determination, teamwork, persistence, integrity, citizenship, justice, and commitment bringing our total back to nine.

I hope you'll be inspired by the stories you read in this book — and that they'll help you dare to imagine your own future!

— Sharon Robinson

COURAGE DETERMINATION

TEAMWORK PERSISTENCE

INTEGRITY CITIZENSHIP

JUSTICE COMMITMENT

EXCELLENCE **JACKIE'S NINE**

DETERMINATION TEAMWORK

PERSISTENCE INTEGRITY

CITIZENSHIP JUSTICE

COMMITMENT EXCELLENCE

EXCELLENCE COURAGE

DETERMINATION TEAMWORK

PERSISTENCE INTEGRITY

COURAGE DETERMINATION

TEAMWORK PERSISTENCE

INTEGRITY CITIZENSHIP

JUSTICE COMMITMENT

EXCELLENCE **COURAGE**

DETERMINATION TEAMWORK

PERSISTENCE INTEGRITY

CITIZENSHIP JUSTICE

COMMITMENT EXCELLENCE

EXCELLENCE COURAGE

DETERMINATION TEAMWORK

PERSISTENCE INTEGRITY

In the Shadow of Your Wings

ONE OF THE MOST HISTORIC MOMENTS in the twentieth century took place five years before I was born. On August 28, 1945, Jackie Robinson and Branch Rickey shook hands in an office at 215 Montague Street in Brooklyn and nothing in the world was ever quite the same again.

It would be eleven years later, as my father's baseball career was coming to a close, before I would even begin to understand what happened that day. And it was not a particularly pleasant experience for me.

I was six. Mom dropped Jackie and me off at our summer day camps in the suburbs of Connecticut. It was raining, so I ran inside the craft shop to find out my group's assignment for the day.

The assembled campers looked like a sea of white faces. Being the only black girl in a group of eighty campers brought the usual pang of insecurity. The fact that we were all dressed in the same uniform, white cotton short-sleeved shirts with the Camp Hilltop/Camp

As a child, I had no idea of the personal sacrifice that was involved in my dad's first couple of years in Major League Baseball until I saw the movie, The Jackie Robinson Story. My father played himself.

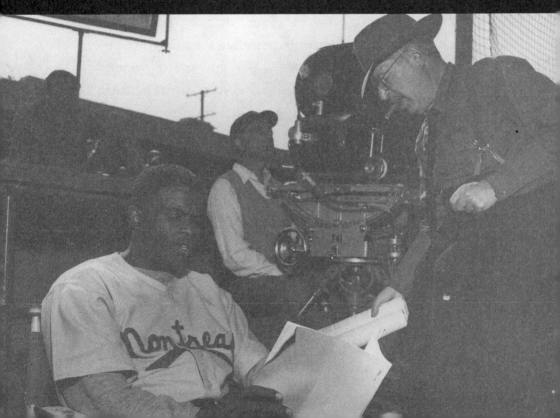

Holloway emblem on the right pocket, and navy blue shorts similarly embossed, did not make up for the feeling that I was different. But I brightened when I recognized a few friends. I ran to join my group. The room was particularly noisy, full of children, prisoners to the wet weather.

The camp directors came to the front of the room, each wearing a red, short-sleeved knit shirt and khaki trousers. After quieting us, they announced that we would rotate between one of four activities: arts and crafts, movies, games, and lunch. My group was selected for the first showing of films.

As the other campers scattered to their assigned activities, a moan went up from some of the kids in my group who recalled the last film festival we'd sat through: *The 5,000 Fingers of Dr. T,* and the original *Cinderella.*

We were instructed to sit on the picnic benches that had been brought in from the outside while two counselors set up the portable movie screen in the front of the room and two others adjusted the 16mm film on the projector. As we settled down, the lights were flicked off and the movie began to roll.

The title of the first film couldn't have shocked me more. It was *The Jackie Robinson Story,* starring Jackie Robinson and Ruby Dee. My eyes opened wide, my heart beat faster, and I had to catch my breath as I tried not to gasp. The girl with whom I shared the bench poked me in the ribs.

I sat frozen, listening to the cheers and whistles from the other kids. Jackie Robinson was a hero even at day camp, and they all knew my connection to him. Once he had even visited the camp for a fireside chat with the campers who were staying on an overnight. He had also arranged for sixty of the older campers to attend a game at Ebbets Field between the Dodgers and the Cincinnati Reds.

The film was in black and white. A young actor portrayed Dad in his youth, but as time and the movie progressed, the younger man was replaced by my father. It was Dad's Hollywood debut, and as I sat in amazement on the hard bench, there he stood, tall and statuesque, looking much younger and thinner than I now knew him. But there was no mistaking that broad smile that could light up my world or those strong hands that could practically encircle my waist. He was so handsome. Studying his clean-shaven face on the screen, I noticed a deep cleft in his chin. The cleft was not so obvious now; his face had become more rounded in his post-baseball days. He smiled again, revealing those perfectly straight, white teeth, which stood out in sharp contrast to his ebony face. I shivered.

Until that day, my familiarity with the movie was pretty much limited to knowledge of its existence.

Mom and Dad had told me the history of the film many times, sometimes placing me as much in the starring role as my father. The story went something like this: I was born two weeks before production was scheduled to begin. After my arrival on January 13, 1950 (duly recorded by the New York papers), Dad and Jackie Jr. left Mom and me in our St. Alban's home, while they flew to Los Angeles for the filming. Soon arrangements were made for us to join them on the West Coast. I took my first plane ride at age three weeks. In Los Angeles, Mom, Jackie, and I made daily visits to the movie set. We have pictures of me in the arms of Ruby Dee, who was playing my mother.

If my knowledge of the film was obscure, my understanding of my father's accomplishments was equally fuzzy. By the time I was born the major trauma of the first few years in baseball were behind my parents. I did not grow up hearing horror stories of my father's pioneering efforts. All I knew was that my dad was a famous baseball player on the Brooklyn Dodgers and that people loved to tell stories about his feats. Dad retired from Major League Baseball when I was six.

Now, I was watching this story about my father for the first time that I could remember in a room filled with white people. I saw a story about his playing, a story of racism and one brave attempt to end an aspect of it. It would have been a peculiar situation for an adult to deal with. It was certainly beyond the powers of comprehension of a six-year-old.

◆   ◆   ◆

My reaction to seeing my father play himself on the big screen was a combination of mortification and pride. Much later, I learned to admire my father's courage and the enormous sacrifice inherent in his decision to adopt the nonviolent approach to social change. Years before Dr. Martin Luther King, Jr. coined the philosophy of nonviolence on American soil, my dad had persevered and won.

The Meeting

by Jules Tygiel

THE MEETING BETWEEN BRANCH RICKEY [President, Brooklyn Dodgers] and Jackie Robinson has passed into the folklore of American sports. Sukeforth [Clyde Sukeforth, Dodgers scout] introduced the two men, warning Rickey that he had not watched Robinson throw. "But the old man was so engrossed in Robinson by that time, he didn't hear a damn word I said," remembers Sukeforth. "When Rickey met somebody he was interested in, he studied them in the most profound way. He just sat and stared. And that's what he did with Robinson — stared at him as if he were trying to get inside the man. And Jack stared right back at him." Robinson also recalls that moment, "His piercing eyes roamed over me with such meticulous care, I almost felt naked."

Rickey saw a good-looking, broad-shouldered man, one half inch shy of six feet tall. Robinson possessed, by one description, "a sensitive, intelligent, face, with strong features, a high forehead, wide and somewhat

Professional sports was racially segregated — until August 28, 1945, when my father, then a shortstop for the Kansas City Monarchs, a Negro League team, signed an agreement that led to the breaking of baseball's infamous color line.

brooding eyes, a full mouth, and determined chin." His skin was uncompromisingly dark. Columnist John Crosby called him, "the blackest black man, as well as one of the handsomest, I ever saw."

Rickey told Robinson of his extensive research into the athlete's career and personal life. He then revealed the purpose of the meeting. Robinson, despite any earlier suspicions, was nonetheless jolted. He also remained skeptical. "It took me a long time to convince myself that Rickey was not just making a gesture," he told Wendell Smith [sports writer]. For three hours, Rickey harangued Robinson on the responsibilities incumbent upon the first black player, graphically illustrating the difficulties that Robinson might face. He portrayed the hostile teammate, the abusive opponent, the insulting fan, the obstinate hotel clerk. Rickey challenged the black man with racial epithets and verbally transplanted him into ugly confrontations. "His acting was so convincing that I found myself chain-gripping my fingers behind my back," wrote Robinson.

In the face of this onslaught Robinson finally responded, "Mr. Rickey, do you want a ballplayer who's afraid to fight back?" The Mahatma had awaited this moment. "I want a player with guts enough not to fight back," he roared.

The purpose of Rickey's theatrics grew apparent to Robinson. When the Dodger president posed as a player who had just punched Robinson in the cheek, the man who had fought Jim Crow in the army replied, "I get it. What you want me to say is that I've got another cheek." Rickey produced a copy of Papini's *Life of Christ* and asked Robinson to read the sections on "Nonresistance." He impressed upon the black athlete the necessity to retreat from all confrontations until he had established himself in the major leagues.

Robinson did not accept the challenge hastily. Sukeforth, the sole witness to this historic meeting, later told Rickey, "I was impressed with the fellow and the way he handled himself. He would not go off half-cocked. He gave your questions serious thought before he answered them." It seemed to Sukeforth like a full five minutes before Robinson responded to Rickey's appeal. The black athlete finally replied, "Mr. Rickey, I think I can play ball in Montreal. I think I can play ball in Brooklyn. But, you're a better judge of that than I am. If you want to take this gamble, I will promise you there will be no incident."

Thus began one of the most remarkable relationships in sports history, one which Rachel Robinson feels people have misunderstood. "The things that have been reported about it make it sound very paternalistic on Mr. Rickey's part as though he directed everything," asserts Rachel. "There was much more of an attitude of their being collaborators and conspirators. . . . There was an alliance between them and a kind of mutual respect."

◆　◆　◆

When given the opportunity to showcase his talents on the national scene and to assume a leadership position in the movement for justice and equality in the United States, my father took his mission seriously. He retaliated against the racism unleashed against him on the playing field by performing with unparalleled excellence. He did it so that the playing field would remain equal and other athletes of color would be included in professional sports. At the end of 1947, my father's first year with the Brooklyn Dodgers, he had maintained a batting average of over .300, finished second in the league in runs scored, and first in bases stolen. He led the Dodgers in home runs and was named Rookie of the Year. His brilliant performance on and off the field helped establish attendance records as fans swelled the stands to witness this historic year in baseball.

She Walked Alone

by Daisy Bates

Dr. Benjamin Fine, Pulitzer Prize-winning education editor of the New York Times, was among the first reporters on the scene to cover the story of the integration of Central High in Little Rock, Arkansas. There he met Elizabeth Eckford. This is his impression of that extraordinary young woman.

Courageous acts by young people are particularly inspiring, because they often carry forth the plan without a full understanding of the circumstances.

◆　◆　◆

ELIZABETH, WHOSE DIGNITY AND CONTROL in the face of jeering mobsters had been filmed by television cameras and recorded in pictures flashed to newspapers over the world, had overnight become a national heroine.

"You remember the day before we were to go in," she said during an interview. "We met Superintendent Blossom at the school board office. He told us what the mob might say and do but he never told us we wouldn't have any protection. He told our parents not to come

On September 4, 1957, Elizabeth Eckford and eight other black students, referred to as the Little Rock Nine, were turned away by the National Guard when they tried to enter high school in Little Rock, Arkansas.

because he wouldn't be able to protect the children if they did."

"That night I was so excited I couldn't sleep. The next morning I was about the first one up. While I was pressing my black and white dress — which I had made to wear on the first day of school — my little brother turned on the TV set. They started telling about a large crowd gathered at the school. . . . She [my mother] was so upset and worried. I wanted to comfort her, so I said, 'Mother don't worry.'

"Dad was walking back and forth, from room to room, with a sad expression. He was chewing on his pipe and he had a cigar in his hand, but he didn't light either one. It would have been funny, only he was so nervous.

"Before I left home Mother called us into the living-room. She said we should have a word of prayer. Then I caught the bus and got off a block from the school. I saw a large crowd of people standing across the street from the soldiers guarding Central. As I walked on, the crowd suddenly got very quiet. Superintendent Blossom had told us to enter by the front door. I looked at all the people and thought, 'Maybe I will be safer if I walk down the block to the front entrance behind the guards.'

"At the corner, I tried to pass through the long line of guards around the school so as to enter the grounds behind them. One of the guards pointed across the street. So I pointed in the same direction and asked whether he meant for me to cross the street and walk down. He nodded 'yes.' So, I walked across the street conscious of the crowd that stood there, but they moved away from me.

"For a moment all I could hear was the shuffling of their feet. Then someone shouted, 'Here she comes, get ready!' I moved away from the crowd on the sidewalk and into the street. If the mob came at me I could then cross back over so the guards could protect me.

"The crowd moved in closer and then began to follow me, calling me names. I still wasn't afraid. Just a little bit nervous. Then my knees started to shake all of a sudden and I wondered whether I could make it to the center entrance a block away. It was the longest block I ever walked in my whole life.

"Even so, I still wasn't too scared because all the time I kept thinking that the guards would protect me.

"When I got right in front of the school, I went up to a guard again. But this time he just looked straight ahead and didn't move to let me pass him. I didn't know what to do. Then I looked and saw that the path leading to the front entrance was a little further ahead. So I walked until I was right in front of the path to the front door.

"I stood looking at the school — it looked so big! Just then the guards let some white students go through.

"The crowd was quiet. I guess they were waiting to see what was going to happen. When I was able to steady my knees, I walked up to the guard who had let the white students in. He too didn't move. When I tried to squeeze past him, he raised his bayonet and then the other guards closed in and they raised their bayonets.

"They glared at me with a mean look and I was very frightened and didn't know what to do. I turned around and the crowd came toward me.

"They moved closer and closer. Somebody started yelling, 'Lynch her! Lynch her!'

"I tried to see a friendly face somewhere in the mob — someone who maybe would help. I looked into the face of an old woman and it seemed a kind face, but when I looked at her again, she spat on me.

"They came closer, shouting, 'No nigger bitch is going to get in our school. Get out of here!'

"I turned back to the guards but their faces told me I wouldn't get help from them. Then I looked down the block and saw a bench at the bus stop. I thought, 'If I can only get there I will be safe.' I don't know why the bench seemed a safe place to me, but I started walking toward it. I tried to close my mind to what they were shouting, and kept saying to myself, 'If I can only make it to the bench I will be safe.'

"When I finally got there, I don't think I could have gone another step. I sat down and the mob crowded up and began shouting all over again. Someone hollered, 'Drag her over to this tree! Let's take care of the nigger.' Just then a white man sat down beside me, put his arm around me and patted my shoulder. He raised my chin and said, 'Don't let them see you cry.'

"Then, a white lady — she was very nice — she came over to me on the bench. She spoke to me but I don't remember now what she said. She put me on the bus and sat next to me. She asked me my name and tried to talk to me but I don't think I answered. I can't remember much about the bus ride, but the next thing I remember I was standing in front of the School for the Blind, where Mother works.

"I thought, 'Maybe she isn't here. But she has to be here!' So I ran upstairs, and I think some teachers tried to talk to me, but I kept running until I reached Mother's classroom.

"Mother was standing at the window with her head bowed, but she must have sensed I was there because she turned around. She looked as if she had been crying, and I wanted to tell her I was all right. But I couldn't speak. She put her arms around me and I cried."

COURAGE DETERMINATION

TEAMWORK PERSISTENCE

INTEGRITY CITIZENSHIP

JUSTICE COMMITMENT

EXCELLENCE COURAGE

DETERMINATION TEAMWORK

PERSISTENCE INTEGRITY

CITIZENSHIP JUSTICE

COMMITMENT EXCELLENCE

EXCELLENCE COURAGE

DETERMINATION TEAMWORK

PERSISTENCE INTEGRITY

The Capping Ceremony

I remember being a teenager and desperately wanting people to see me only as Sharon and not as Jackie Robinson's daughter. The problem was I had no idea who Sharon was. I decided to explore, and even reject and run from my prescribed identity until I discovered me. So, when the time came, I consciously applied to Howard University under my married name, ignoring the lines that asked for my parents' names. After I had successfully completed my sophomore year I was ready to merge my two identities.

◆   ◆   ◆

I ARRIVED AT RANKIN CHAPEL dressed for the first time in our Howard University student-nurse uniforms, a starched, blue-and-white pinstriped dress with a round navy blue collar covered by a white apron that buttoned on either side, white stockings, and brand-new white oxford nursing shoes.

We assembled in the lower level of the chapel, lined up by height. There were about thirty members of the class of 1973; a fairly diverse group in terms of age,

My father died during my senior year, which made his presence at my capping cere-
mony earlier all the more special. When I graduated, I tossed my mortarboard high up
in the sky, knowing Dad was up there smiling down on me.

marital status, and even nationality. Our common link-age was our collective African descent and our desire and determination to become nurses.

Nervous with expectation, I clutched my white candle tightly as we proceeded in pairs up the stairs and into the stained-glass chapel. The room was packed. As my eyes adjusted to the dim lighting, I spotted my mother and father sitting in the middle section. Dad was at the end of the aisle.

When I applied to Howard I did so using my married name. Prior to the capping ceremony, I had remained determined to maintain my anonymity. To do so meant talking about my parents to my classmates and friends at school only in general terms and asking a few close friends not to disclose my secret. I lived off campus, held down a part-time job, and socialized mostly with students outside of nursing. So, for the first twelve months at Howard, I moved freely about the student body without fear of being singled out because of my parents' fame.

On this night of celebration, though, I no longer felt the need to hide. As I marched across the stage the night of the capping ceremonies I knew that by the end of the evening I would still be Sharon, but I would also be Jackie Robinson's daughter. I felt a tremendous sense of relief to be able to equally embrace both.

After the formal part of the ceremony came to a

close, my classmates and I scattered in search of family and friends. I rushed joyously into my parents' arms, happy and carefree as a five-year-old at her birthday party. Mom, Dad, and I joined the receiving line and waited our turn to greet the faculty. Although I pretended not to notice, I felt the stares, heard the whispers, and recognized the confusion. We were next in line.

"Dean Coles, I'd like you to meet my parents, Jack and Rachel Robinson." I spoke without taking my eyes off Dean Cole's face. She was known for being dramatic. I wondered how she would play this scene. A striking, elegant woman who stood nearly six feet tall, her eyes looked into my father's directly.

"I'm very pleased to meet you both," she said, remaining gracious and poised, and giving in only slightly to her delight at having a celebrity in her midst. As soon as the receiving line broke, Dean Coles approached with a photographer and our mutual good feeling was photographically preserved.

My mother told me after the ceremony that on the way down to Washington my father acted as though he were going to the coronation of the queen. For me, it was a coming out party equal to the most elaborate cotillion, Bar Mitzvah or African rites of passage ceremony. And, in retrospect, it proved to be all the more important because it was the last of my milestones that my father would live to see.

DETERMINATION

Breaking the Color Barrier

by Jackie Robinson

A FEW WEEKS AFTER THE WEDDING, we were to fly to Daytona Beach, Florida, where I was to report for spring training with the Montreal farm club. We started out by plane from Los Angeles, arriving at New Orleans quite early in the morning. Upon arrival, I was told to go into the terminal. Rachel waited and waited. Then the stewardess came up to her and suggested that she go into the terminal and take all her things with her. I discovered we had been bumped from our flight owing to military priorities, so they said. We were not alarmed, having been assured that there would be only a brief delay. But as we argued our rights, our plane took off. Another typical black experience. After a few hours we weren't as concerned about the time we were losing as we were about the hunger we felt. Blacks could not eat in the coffee shop but could take food out. We asked where we could find a restaurant. We learned there was one that would prepare sandwiches provided we did not sit down and eat them there. Though we were both

That first spring training with the Brooklyn Dodgers' farm team in Montreal, my parents had to cope with being newlyweds and battle the indignities of racial prejudice and discrimination. Surviving this experience helped prepare them for the challenges ahead.

weary and hungry, we decided to skip food until we reached a place where we could be treated as human beings.

Our next project was to find a hotel where we could wait until we got another flight. The only accommodations were in a filthy, run-down place resembling a flophouse. A roof over our heads and a chance to lie down, even in a bed of uncertain sanitary condition, was better than nothing. We made the best of it and notified the airport where we could be found. They promised to call. They did. At seven in the evening, exactly twelve hours after we had been told about a "brief delay," we were in the air again. After a short flight, the plane set down at Pensacola, Florida, for fueling. The manager of the Pensacola Airport told me that we were being bumped again. There wasn't any explanation this time. They had simply put a white couple in our seats. A black porter managed to get us a limousine. It stopped at a hotel in Pensacola, and the white driver summoned a black bellboy and asked him where we could get room and board for the night. The bellboy recommended the home of a black family. They were generous and warmhearted people who insisted on taking us in, in spite of the fact that they had a huge family and a tiny home. Their willingness to share made us forget about being sorry for ourselves. Realistically, though, there was just no room for us. We thanked them, telling them we couldn't dream of inconveniencing them and got a ride to the Greyhound bus terminal. We had decided to take the next bus to Jacksonville, thinking that at least we could relax a bit and rest our backs, but we were in for another rude jolt. We had sunk down gratefully into a couple of seats and pushed the little buttons which move you back into a reclining position. The bus was empty when we boarded, and we had taken seats in the middle of the bus. I fell fast asleep. At the first stop, a crowd of passengers got on. The bus driver gestured to us, indicated that we were to move to the back of the bus. The seats at the back were reserved seats — reserved for Negroes — and they were straight-backed. No little button to push. No reclining seats.

I had a bad few seconds, deciding whether I could continue to endure this humiliation. After we had been bumped a second time at the Pensacola Airport, I had been ready to explode with rage, but I knew that the result would mean newspaper headlines about an ugly racial incident and possible arrest not only for me but also for Rae. By giving in to my feelings then, I could have blown the whole major league bit. I had swallowed my pride and choked back my anger. Again, this time it would have been easier to take a beating than to remain passive. But I remembered the things Rae and I had said to each other during the months we had tried to prepare ourselves for exactly this kind of ordeal. We had agreed that I had no right to lose my temper and jeopardize the chances of all the blacks who would follow me if I could help break down the barriers. So we moved back to the very last seat as indicated by the driver. The bus continued to pick up passengers. They came on board the bus and filled up the choice white seats. The black section was so crowded that every other person sat forward on the edge to create more room. In the dark, Rachel was quietly crying, but I didn't know that until years later. She was crying for me and not out of self-pity. She felt badly because she knew I felt helpless. She hoped I realized that she knew how much strength it took to take these injustices and not strike back.

DETERMINATION

Still Me

by Christopher Reeve

*Christopher Reeve, the man who once portrayed a hero with super-
human capability, has had to find superhuman strength to carry on
with his life following a fall while horseback riding. Although par-
alyzed, he, his wife Dana, and their three children, Will, Matthew,
and Alexandra all maintain hope that this true superman will one
day walk again.*

◆　◆　◆

[DURING MY HOSPITALIZATION] at UVA [University of
Virginia] and at Kessler [rehabilitation center], I always
kept the picture of the Pyramid of Quetzalcoatl in
front of me. I would look at the hundreds of steps leading up to the clouds and imagine myself climbing
slowly but surely to the top. That desire sustained me in
the early days after my injury, but during the next couple of years I had to learn to face the reality: you man-
age to climb one or two steps, but then something
happens and you fall back three. The worst of it is the

Christopher Reeve received a standing ovation when he appeared at the 1996 Academy Awards. He has dedicated his life to increasing the public's awareness of spinal cord injuries and to advancing the science surrounding this field. His determination, his courage, his faith are awesome.

unpredictability. Several times I've made a commitment to appear at a function or give a speech, but the night before, or even that morning, a skin tear, or dysreflexia, or a lung infection suddenly developed and I had to go to the hospital instead.

Climbing up the steps, I've appeared at the Oscars, spoken at the Democratic Convention, directed a film, written this book, worked on political issues, and traveled more extensively than most high-level quadriplegics. But falling backwards, I've been hospitalized eleven times for dysreflexia, pneumonia, a collapsed lung, a broken arm, two blood clots, a possible hip fracture, and the infection in my left ankle that nearly resulted in the partial amputation of my leg.

I was told by so many "experts" — doctors, psychologists, physical therapists, other patients, and well-meaning friends and family members — that as time went by not only would I become more stable physically but I would become well adjusted psychologically to my condition. I have found exactly the opposite to be true. The longer you sit in a wheelchair, the more the body breaks down and the harder you have to fight against it. Psychologically, I feel I have established a workable baseline: I have my down days, but I haven't been incapacitated by them. This doesn't mean, though, that I accept paralysis, or that I'm at peace with it.

The sensory deprivation hurts the most: I haven't

been able to give my son Will a hug since he was two years old, and now he's five and a half. . . . The physical world is still very meaningful to me; I have not been able to detach myself from it and live entirely in my mind. I'm jealous when someone talks about a recent skiing vacation, when friends embrace each other, or even when Will plays hockey in the driveway with someone else.

If someone were to ask me what is the most difficult lesson I've learned from all this, I'm very clear about it: I know I have to give when sometimes I really want to take. I've realized instinctively that it's part of my job as a father now not to cause Will to worry about me. If I were to give in to self-pity or express my anger in front of him, it would place an unfair burden on this carefree five-year-old. If I were to turn inward and spend my time mourning the past, I couldn't be as close to Matthew and Alexandra, two teenagers who naturally need to turn to me for advice. And what kind of life would it be for Dana if I let myself go and became just a depressed hulk in a wheelchair? All of this takes effort on my part, because it's still very difficult to accept the turn my life has taken, simply because of one unlucky moment.

COURAGE DETERMINATION

TEAMWORK PERSISTENCE

INTEGRITY CITIZENSHIP

JUSTICE COMMITMENT

EXCELLENCE COURAGE

DETERMINATION **TEAMWORK**

PERSISTENCE INTEGRITY

CITIZENSHIP JUSTICE

COMMITMENT EXCELLENCE

EXCELLENCE COURAGE

DETERMINATION TEAMWORK

PERSISTENCE INTEGRITY

TEAMWORK

Breaking Barriers

"Right now I am worried about my family. My mom is planning to break up with my dad and my mom will take me and move to a hotel. My dad will take my sister and move. I feel like I am lost in a wide-open place and nobody can find me and bring me home. Like on a baseball field, but no one can see me.

"I would like to have courage, like Jackie Robinson. He was good at not listening to people call him names. When people threw trash on the field, he pretended not to see it. I want to be like this when my dad hits me and my mom tries to protect me by fighting back. I will be glad when this is over."

—an excerpt from a winning *Breaking Barriers* essay

◆　◆　◆

WHEN I READ THE PASSAGE above, I felt tears coming on. The two powerful paragraphs were from an essay written by a student as part of the *Breaking Barriers* program. The program had helped this eleven-year-old, Matt (not his real name), learn an incredible lesson about

In the Breaking Barriers *program, we say that teamwork wins the game. And we're all on the team: you, me, and everyone whose lives we touch.*

courage and about the importance of sharing your problems with someone you trust. In this child's case it was his sixth grade teacher, Suzanne (also not a real name). Suzanne teamed up with other professionals to help Matt and his family.

I first came to know Matt because his essay was one of three Suzanne had attached to a letter asking St. Louis Cardinal Mark McGwire to visit her classroom in San Diego. Ever since the homerun chase, McGwire and Sammy Sosa were on the mind of every 11 year old. Because of Major League Baseball's *Breaking Barriers* program, Suzanne copied me on the letter.

Suzanne's students, most of whom have learning or neurological disorders, were working on the *Breaking Barriers* curriculum. As part of the program, the children had written essays about barriers they face. Clearly Matt was facing some pretty tough — and danger- ous — obstacles.

I called Suzanne in San Diego to find out how she had dealt with Matt's disturbing revelations. As the phone rang, I thought about the load today's teachers have to bear. So much is expected of them, and, un- fortunately, so few are properly rewarded for coping with these enormous responsibilities.

After talking with Suzanne for just five minutes, I sighed, completely at ease. Her warmth, competence, and sincerity came through immediately. I listened as she described the intervention plan that had taken place since Matt put his problem into print. I thanked Suzanne for getting help for this child, but words alone seemed inadequate. I promised then and there to come visit Matt's class in the spring and bring a baseball player with me. I couldn't bring McGwire, since he was on the St. Louis team, but I already had a player in mind, a San Diego Padres player, with an investment in the community.

Suzanne and I talked a couple of times over the next few months. She kept me posted on Matt's progress. I worked with the Padres staff to include Matt's class in our *Breaking Barriers* spring tour.

Meanwhile, by the March 15 deadline, we'd received nearly 2,000 entries for the *Breaking Barriers* essay contest. The essays were organized by city and then judged by a team of editors at Scholastic publishers, who sent a list of finalists to my office. I assembled a team with representatives from Scholastic, Major League Baseball, and the Major League Baseball Players Association. We started reading.

When we reached the essay finalists from San Diego, I was thrilled to see that Matt's work was still in the running. And why not? His essay was well structured, his obstacle was clearly defined, he talked about the value of courage, and had concluded his essay with a powerful analogy comparing his father hitting him to my dad facing a fast ball.

As we began tallying the votes, I held my breath not wanting to unjustly influence the vote. The count was unanimous. Matt was the grand prizewinner for San Diego!

The *Breaking Barriers* spring tour lasts from mid-April until mid-June. With 22 Major League Baseball cities participating in the program that year, I had to narrow the list of cities we could actually visit in that time period. As it turned out San Diego was the tenth city on our seven-week tour.

I arrived in San Diego psyched about meeting Matt. I knew it was going to be a powerful visit, especially since the Padres and Allyne Price, my partner from the Major League Baseball Players Association, had arranged for Tony Gwynn to join us. Tony Gwynn: power hitter and baseball legend! I mean *I* was excited.

May 26, 2000, I woke up ready, but a bit nervous. I wanted everything to go just right for this teacher and child.

I arrived at Matt's school around ten and found out that Tony Gwynn had come early. I thanked Tony for coming and talked briefly about our goal for the day. It was then that I learned that he'd already bonded with Matt by spending time alone with him before I arrived.

As Tony and I headed into the school, this frail, but beaming child came bouncing down the stairs toward us. I knew instantly that this was Matt. I gathered him in my arms like an old friend and my concerns for the day faded completely. The boy was already happy.

Our arrival immediately thrust Matt into hero status among his classmates and we did everything in our power to make his legend grander. Our first stop, after the principal's office, was to Suzanne's class for some private time. Then, we went to the auditorium for an assembly for the entire sixth grade. By then television cameras has also arrived and Matt's star status was bumped up a notch!

As usual, I opened the assembly by sharing stories about my dad that focused on his character. After getting the students' input on how they defined the term barriers, the talk shifted to how to deal with them. I then asked Tony Gwynn if he had anything he wanted to share with the kids. Tony jumped right in, holding all of us captive with stories from his trials and tribulations as a professional ballplayer. His most recent obstacle was a series of injuries that threatened his career.

Tony and I fielded the usual questions: What was it like to be Jackie Robinson's daughter? How do you hit a fast ball? But the students also wanted to know more about my personal barriers.

Given the courage Matt had already displayed, I felt

compelled to tell the kids about a personal barrier I'd faced as a teenager. "I was eighteen when I heard over the radio that my older brother, Jackie, had been arrested for drugs and arms possession." I began, voice soft. "Seeing Jackie behind bars shocked me into accepting that I'd lost control of my life, too. You see," I continued maintaining eye contact with the students. "I was engaged to marry a man who abused me."

The room was dead silent. I moved quickly on to the values I'd used to help me support my brother and get myself out of an abusive relationship. "I've overcome barriers of my own. And, that's why we're here today."

Finally the questions shifted to baseball technique. Tony got physical with his response. He assumed his batting stance, pretended to grip a bat, and went into full swing. As Tony carried through to complete the swing, I thought of the analogy in Anthony's essay: "my sister is fourteen and she says that sometimes you have to just look straight at him. I will try to do this next time, like Jackie Robinson looks at a fast ball. Only he's doing the hitting. I think courage will be easier when I'm a man." Wow! I thought as Tony talked about the power and focus necessary to connect to the ball.

I noticed that Matt had begun to fidget. I worried that he, too, had just made the same connection with that passage from his essay. I was so wrong. Matt leaned over to me and whispered, "I can't wait 'til tonight when I'm on that field." I hugged him and smiled. As the essay contest's grand prizewinner for San Diego, Matt had won Padres' tickets for his entire class and three members of his family. But, he wasn't thinking about the game, either. Matt was already imagining himself on the field, being honored during the pregame ceremony.

After the assembly was over, Suzanne and I talked quietly for a few minutes. She told me that Matt's parents had separated; that, no, Matt hadn't invited his father to the game. And, yes he was doing well in school and in life. I felt so good about our *Breaking Barriers* program, about this wonderful teacher, about the commitment demonstrated by the Padres and about Tony Gwynn's integrity and compassion. Then, I thought about my dad and the lessons he'd taught me. I was now sharing Dad's values with hundreds of thousands of kids across the United States and Canada. Teamwork, I thought, teamwork had helped change this one little boy's life.

The Colonel from "Old Kaintuck"

by Carl Rowan

In the eighties, Whitney Houston recorded One Moment in Time *as a tribute to Olympians. In it, she sings about the importance of believing in yourself and seizing your moment. Leaders often emerge out of one of these special moments. Sometimes that moment is dependent upon your talent; other times it requires your taking a stand on an important issue. Pee Wee Reese, the Dodgers' captain, my father's teammate, and a white Southerner, seized such a moment. He faced the hostile, racist jeering of a raucous baseball stadium crowd and bravely showed that he understood that the Dodgers' success depended upon his leadership — and all of them working as a team.*

◆ ◆ ◆

IN 1949, 1950 AND 1951, when Robinson was at his peak and his every hour was filled with the world's acclaim, he was quick to say, with no pretense of modesty, that he had not gotten that far alone. There were Branch Rickey, Clay Hopper, Rae, Lester Granger and a host of other people who had boosted him over barrier

During a tense game between the Boston Braves and the Brooklyn Dodgers, Pee Wee Reese (second from left) left his position and put his arm around my father. That simple act helped solidify one of the most incredible sports' teams of the 20th century.

after barrier, given him courage when his troubles seemed all-consuming. There was one man who, unlike all these, had no personal interest of any sort in seeing that Robinson made good, but who, nevertheless, had been a prime figure in Jackie's development. That man was Pee Wee Reese, the Dodger shortstop.

Robinson had held up under the mental strain of 1947 and played baseball of major league caliber largely because of Reese, the "Kentucky colonel" whose decency and courage in seemingly insignificant situations had buoyed him up and kept him believing that America is populated mainly by decent people who justify the Negro's continued optimism. Not that Reese was a crusader, a lecturer about the heritage of freedom or the rights of a minority, or the necessity for baseball to operate on a democratic basis; actually, when Robinson joined the Dodgers in 1947, Reese was a puckish-faced young man of twenty-seven who looked as if he had just been munching on a green persimmon, and as if he were much too young to be playing baseball in the majors. Yet it was Reese more than anyone who led Robinson to believe that a courageous man is the noblest work of God — not a man of physical courage, for some of the most daring physical feats in history have been the work of fools, but a man of moral courage. Robinson soon saw that courage was what Pee Wee had, although the two had played together for years, had become one of the greatest keystone combinations in the history of baseball, before Robinson realized fully how much courage it had required for Reese to treat him as just another ballplayer and to insist in his own way that others do the same.

Actually, Reese was thrust under moral and social pressure from the day Robinson signed a Montreal contract, for that day a newspaperman located Reese to get his views on the signing of a Negro. Reese was thoughtful for a while, then he asked the newspaperman whimsically: "What position did you say this guy played?"

"Shortstop."

"Well, that's the old Reese luck for you. There're nine positions and this guy has to play shortstop."

Pee Wee watched the writer's face, noting that he seemed to take this remark as denoting fear by Reese that Robinson might get his job. "However," added Reese, "there may be room enough in baseball for both of us."

The incident Robinson remembers best as illustrating Reese's innate decency occurred in Boston, however, shortly after Jackie was shifted to second base. The Boston bench jockeys decided that rather than give Robinson the works, they would goad Reese — and possibly knock off two horses with one bit of jockeying.

"Hey, Pee Wee, you and your pal going to dinner together tonight?" someone would shout as the Dodgers took infield practice.

"Hey out there, Kentucky boy. When yo' grand-pappy finds out how you up heah socializing and frat-ernizing with cullud folks he's gonna cut you off from yo' mint juleps," another player bellowed.

For a while Reese ignored the calls, spitting in the pocket of his glove and pounding it with his fist while staring straight ahead. As the calls got louder, however, he strode over to Robinson and put his arm around his shoulder. They talked for a minute in buddy–buddy fashion — oddly enough, neither Robinson nor Reese remembers a single word they said — and the Braves' players fell silent. Reese had said, simply but with force: Robinson and I are teammates, and we came here to play baseball. We came to beat the living daylights out of Boston. If the Braves want to spend their time throwing silly barbs while we play baseball, that's all right with us. That ended the race heckling.

TEAMWORK
Together Now! PUSH!

by David Robinson

My brother David owns a coffee farm in Tanzania, East Africa, and heads a coffee cooperative of over 200 farmers. When he first announced that he was moving to Africa, I resisted his decision. Having recently lost my father and older brother, I felt that David should remain close to home. But when my brother set off for another continent, my mother and I rejoiced at his courage.

David has now lived in Tanzania for nearly two decades. And, because we're such a close family, we've found ways to bridge the geographic separation. David comes home twice a year and my mother makes semi-annual trips to Tanzania to visit our African family. In January of 2000, I made the trip with my mother. We joined David and his young daughters, Meta, Rachel, Liah, and Faith on a wonderful safari. We traveled in a jeep across the Serengeti Plains and into the Ngorogoro crater in search of animals. At night my nieces entertained us with imaginative stories told in Swahili.

As it turned out ten days wasn't long enough for us to include a visit to David's farm so I asked him to write an essay about his work and decision to name the farm Sweet Unity.

◆ ◆ ◆

David's farm, Sweet Unity, is part of a larger cooperative in Tanzania, East Africa. My brother took time away from farming to join Mom and I on safari. It was such a treat to have my nieces, Rachel, Faith, Liah, and Meta along.

SWEET UNITY FARMS lies on 120 acres in the Southern Highlands of Tanzania, East Africa.

We grow coffee and along with our neighbors we ship our coffee to America for sale.

Eleven years ago the land was thickly covered with trees. It was the forest on the far outskirts of our village. I asked permission and the village council agreed to let me establish my family's farm within that forest. For months our fifteen-man team, led by my son, left the village on foot early each morning with axes, hoes, and shovels. Slowly the trees were cut down and their deep roots dug up. Week by week, acre by acre, the forest was being pushed aside and the rolling landscape lay ready for new planting. Our fifteen men walking in single file, often in silence, fifteen men heading to accomplish one task. The walk gave me time to see and think and feel. As I brought up the rear of the line I looked ahead and saw men of the Makonde and Wazaramu tribes from the coast of Tanzania; Wanyamwezi people from Central Tanzania; and my son, Howard, an African-American, from New York.

All men of my race, who had agreed to move together, to labor with one purpose; to toil until the land was open and fresh and planted with thousands of six-inch coffee seedlings. In the early morning, with feet moving quietly in unison, I felt that which I named our farm. The sweetness of unity. The thrill of many coming together to act as one.

The sweetness of unity is a feeling which can be experienced in any part of the world, but I have known it most often during my life in Africa, a land where the machine does not dominate, where the dynamics of physical existence can be difficult. Most often the starter on my ancient Land Rover does not work. The car requires three men pushing and a driver to jump-start the engine. During the rainy season, sections of our roads can become a mire of slippery mud and rut. Everyone is familiar with the experience of getting stuck. Engine whining, tires spinning and sliding. All able-bodied men out of the vehicle shoulders, hands and backs up against the car's body; all ready for the loud call of one man "Together now! Push!" "Put your strength into it! Push!" Foot by foot, the engine screaming, the men straining, the car moves forward. How many times have I reached home covered to the knees in mud, but proud that together we had not let conditions stop us.

From the time I was a youth growing up in Connecticut, to these days as a farmer in Tanzania, I have seen the merit and often the necessity of joining hands to achieve a goal. Unity is often not a state reached easily, but the inability to achieve it can often mean failure. Coming together at times is not fun, but in a shared success there can be great joy and pride. Sometimes it may be a small thing accomplished. Sometimes it may be survival itself.

Be ready, my children, when you hear the call. In this world it is always riding across the wind, "Together now! PUSH!"

COURAGE DETERMINATION

TEAMWORK PERSISTENCE

INTEGRITY CITIZENSHIP

JUSTICE COMMITMENT

EXCELLENCE COURAGE

DETERMINATION TEAMWORK

PERSISTENCE INTEGRITY

CITIZENSHIP JUSTICE

COMMITMENT EXCELLENCE

EXCELLENCE COURAGE

DETERMINATION TEAMWORK

PERSISTENCE INTEGRITY

PERSISTENCE
Getting Beyond Average

FROM THE TIME WE ENTERED Dolan Junior High, [my best friends] Christy, Candy, and I encountered challenges that we hadn't anticipated. To begin with, I tested poorly on the admission test and was placed in one of the lowest academic groupings. Each group was assigned a number that fell somewhere between one and ten. It didn't take much to figure out that Group 7-7, the one I was assigned to, was for the below-average students. Christy and Candy were placed in the accelerated classes, and I was embarrassed by my ascribed status as a mediocre student.

Inspired by Maria in the movie *West Side Story,* I insisted on taking Spanish the fall of ninth grade. This was a problem for my guidance counselor because I was assigned to Group 9-7. Foreign languages were allowed only for students in groups above four. Remembering the misunderstood Maria, I held my ground as if the Romance language held the key to my salvation, or at least to my first love.

My early years were filled with examples of people who were motivated to change their circumstances in spite of any obstacles. In junior high school I really understood their lessons and put them into action.

My guidance counselor's efforts to convince me that I was not ready for a foreign language fell on deaf ears. Unwilling to accept her decision, I went home and complained to my mother. Incensed, my mother stormed into the school to stand up for me. Her presence made the difference. I was moved up three groups and allowed to take Introductory Spanish.

For the first time, I felt challenged. My grades and class participation improved to meet the higher expectations. I was, however, disappointed to learn that there was only one Puerto Rican boy in my class. When my teacher asked for volunteers to tutor the recent immigrant, I jumped at the opportunity, thinking that maybe this was my "Tony." Well, love was not our destiny, but his English improved and my learning of Spanish was enhanced. More important, for the first time in my school years, I thought of myself as a good student. It was not the same as being smart, but it was certainly better than being average.

PERSISTENCE

Wait 'Til Next Year

by Jackie Robinson

Whether my father's goal was stealing a base, opening a black-controlled bank, or influencing the political and social climate, he fought until the obstacle was removed. My father showed this same persistence when he pushed to complete his autobiography before he died. Again, focus and commitment saw him through. I Never Had It Made *was released a few weeks before my father died.*

◆　◆　◆

DURING THE 1955 SEASON I played in approximately two-thirds of the games. My batting average was down. I was doing a poor job in comparison to past seasons. The newspapers began subtly — and some not so subtly — to refer to me as a has-been.

However, despite this the team made it into the World Series. It was the fifth series we had been in during my 9 seasons with the Dodgers. (We had been in only a total of 7 since 1905 and we had never won one.)

After five World Series attempts, the 1955 Brooklyn Dodgers finally defeated their crosstown rivals, the New York Yankees. There were two milestones that year. The 1955 Dodger squad was the first and only Brooklyn Dodger team to win a World Series championship.

There was a saying in Brooklyn which everyone has heard about the Dodgers ("the bums"): "Wait 'til next year." Well, here we were in our seventh World Series in fifty years and there was hope that this would be the year, but our fans were also ready to shrug their shoulders and say "Wait 'til next year" if we lost. The way we were playing in that first game — down 6–4 in the eighth inning — it looked like we might have to wait. I was on third base and I knew I might not be playing next year. There were two men out, and I suddenly decided to shake things up. It was not the best baseball strategy to steal home with our team two runs behind, but I just took off and did it. I really didn't care whether I made it or not . . . and we came close to winning that first game. Whether it was because of my stealing home or not, the team had new fire. We fought back against our old rivals, the powerful "Bronx Bombers," and the series came down to the wire in the seventh game. Podres pitched a brilliant shutout, and in the sixth inning with men on first and second and only one out Sandy Amoros saved the game with a spectacular running catch of Yogi Berra's fly ball down the left field line. It was one of the greatest thrills of my life to be finally on a World Series winner.

PERSISTENCE

The Great One

by Bruce Markusen

Roberto Walker Clemente played baseball with a passion that was matched only by the community service he performed for his beloved Puerto Rico. He was a man of conscience and commitment. I never met Roberto, but I worked closely with his wife, Vera, and their son, Luis, to help strengthen Clemente's dream of a sports city complex in his home, Carolina, Puerto Rico. Sports City exists today but it has yet to reach its full potential or satisfy Clemente's dream. We're committed to changing that.

Because of Roberto Clemente's stellar performance on and off the field, he remains in the hearts of people around the world forever. Roberto was persistant in all things because he believed his efforts made a difference. His final act of unselfishness and commitment came just after the fans celebrated his 3,000th career hit.

◆ ◆ ◆

ON DECEMBER 23, [1972], A MASSIVE earthquake devastated the Nicaraguan capitol of Managua. The earthquake killed over 7,000 people, while injuring several

For 18 seasons, Roberto Clemente was an opposing pitcher's nightmare and a defensive wizard in the outfield. He won an astonishing 12 consecutive Gold Glove awards and led the Pirates to two World Series victories. In 1973, he was inducted into the Baseball Hall of Fame.

thousand. Damage to residential homes and office buildings mounted, leaving over 25,000 people homeless.

At the suggestion of two acquaintances, [Roberto] Clemente decided to head up a special Puerto Rican committee to collect relief supplies. "Roberto was the leader of the whole mission," recalls Luis Mayoral. "And this came to be maybe a day or two before I last saw him, when the earthquakes really hit. Two television personalities, Luis Vigoreaux — he was a show host in Puerto Rico — and Ruth Fernandez — she's one of the greatest singers ever on the island — they convinced Clemente to go on TV and address the people in Puerto Rico to get together and help send relief supplies for the people damned by the earthquake. That's when Roberto took over unofficially as the leader of that whole movement."

Why would Clemente — or anyone for that matter — undertake such a massive project, especially at a time of year when most people would have been excused for showing a preference to stay with their families? Clemente could have donated money, like most other celebrities, and left the organization of the relief effort to politicians or charitable organizations. So why did Clemente forsake all of his winter plans for the citizens of another country? For one reason, Clemente was not like most other people. He believed in hands-on participation, rather than mere gestures of good will. For another, Clemente had developed a special relationship with Nicaraguan fans during his managerial tour in November. "That's where he kind of fell in love with the people in Nicaragua," maintains Luis Mayoral. "We lost some very good friends in the earthquake," Vera Clemente told Douglas McDaniel of *The Diamond* in 1993. "We met some very nice people there, made friends." In particular, Roberto had become attached to a 14-year-old Nicaraguan orphan who had lost both of his legs. Clemente worried about the fate of the young boy, whom he had arranged to be supplied with artificial limbs.

As the honorary chairman of the earthquake committee, Clemente appeared on local radio and television stations to appeal for food, clothing and other supplies. Putting in 14-hour days, Clemente worked on Christmas Eve, all day on Christmas Day, and then again on the 26th. He committed himself so fully to the effort that he regularly refused meals, barely slept, and never opened the Christmas presents that he had received. He even visited houses in the wealthier sections of San Juan — literally going door to door — asking homeowners to make donations. Spearheaded by Clemente, the committee raised over $150,000 in funds. The relief team also gathered 26 tons of food, clothing and medicine — some of which were donated by the carload — storing them temporarily at Hiram Bithorn Stadium in Santurce.

Clemente also made arrangements to obtain a plane from a company in Miami. The company agreed to lease the plane, for three trips, at a cost of $11,000. In addition to coordinating three successful flights to Nicaragua, the committee organized the voyage of a large shipping vessel filled with goods. Clemente talked of boarding one of the flights personally, but Luis Vigoreaux and Ruth Fernandez discouraged him, citing the uncertain conditions of small cargo planes.

Clemente then received a desperate request from Managua for additional loads of sugar and medical supplies. Clemente agreed to lease another plane, an aging propeller-driven DC-7, for $4,000. When Clemente heard reports that goods targeted for the people of Managua had been intercepted by the Nicaraguan army, he became infuriated. "The Great One" elected to personally accompany the delivery of supplies to Managua.

Clemente and four other men boarded the plane on New Year's Eve. The group included Arturo Rivera — the president of the company that owned the plane — pilot Jerry Hill, flight engineer Francisco Matias, and a man named Rafael Lozano, a friend of Clemente. Several people, including Vera Clemente and teammate Jose Pagan, had expressed concerns about the old plane, which seemed dangerously overloaded. The eight tons of relief supplies were also unevenly distributed, creating a perilous imbalance once the plane left the ground. "Don't do it," said Pagan, one of the Pirates whom Clemente often confided in. "You know everything about baseball, but very little about airplanes." Rivera claimed the aircraft was safe and declared that he would co-pilot the flight to Managua. Influenced by Rivera, Clemente insisted on boarding the plane.

Knowing that she would not return home until the late hours, Vera had dropped her three sons off at her mother's house, where they would stay overnight. Earlier in the day, seven-year-old Roberto, Jr., the oldest of the three boys, had begged his father not to make the trip. The young boy predicted that the plane would not make it to Managua. That evening, in the hours before the flight departed, Roberto, Jr. repeated the premonition to his grandmother. "Grandma, grandma, Daddy is leaving for Nicaragua, and he's not coming back," the young boy cried out. "The plane is going to crash. He's not coming back anymore. I know it. Call mama and don't let him go." Roberto's father, Melchor, had endured a similar nightmare a few nights earlier. In November, Roberto himself had envisioned his own funeral in a dream. "He was always saying that he was going to die young, very young," Vera said.

Vera's mother thought about calling the airport, but

given the lateness of the hour, decided against it. The flight was originally scheduled to leave at four o'clock in the morning, but troubles with the plane delayed the departure until five o'clock in the afternoon. Assuming that the flight was finally about to depart, Vera kissed Roberto goodbye, and drove to an airline terminal to meet some friends who had flown in from the states. From there, Vera returned to Rio Piedras, thinking that Roberto's plane had taken off.

As the plane taxied down the runway, however, more mechanical problems were found. The delay continued for hours. Finally, at 9:20 P.M., the DC-7 took off under normal weather conditions from San Juan International Airport. As the plane lifted off, an airport employee heard one of the plane's four engines vibrating "excessively." Shortly after takeoff, pilot Jerry Hill sensed trouble with one of the engines, which had caught fire. Hill tried to return to the airport, attempting an abrupt left-hand turn. Watching from the ground, a man named Jose Antonio Paris heard an explosion as the plane neared the water's edge. "There were three more explosions after that," Paris said, offering a rare eyewitness description. After the second explosion, co-pilot Arturo Rivera mistakenly retracted the plane's flaps instead of the landing gear. At 9:23 P.M., another explosion occurred as the plane plunged nose-first into the Atlantic Ocean, about a mile and a half from the shore. Within five minutes, the plane had completely submerged. In the meantime, Vera Clemente, unaware of what was transpiring, continued her work at the earthquake committee's headquarters.

Initial media reports said only that Roberto Clemente and the other passengers were "missing." Within hours, such cautious optimism gave way to somber reality. Two and a half hours before the start of the New Year, Robert Walker Clemente was dead — at the age of 38.

COURAGE DETERMINATION

TEAMWORK PERSISTENCE

INTEGRITY CITIZENSHIP

JUSTICE COMMITMENT

EXCELLENCE COURAGE

DETERMINATION TEAMWORK

PERSISTENCE **INTEGRITY**

CITIZENSHIP JUSTICE

COMMITMENT EXCELLENCE

EXCELLENCE COURAGE

DETERMINATION TEAMWORK

PERSISTENCE INTEGRITY

INTEGRITY Love and War

I STILL REMEMBER my grandmother, Zellee Isum's disappointment when I refused to participate in her club's spring cotillion. Considering how much I loved to go to parties, Grandma was correct to think that I would be tempted by the cotillion. On the surface, it was nothing more than a grand party. She tried a quiet sell approach with cautious optimism: the romantic evening, a full-length gown, waltzing with a handsome escort, the before and after parties, my name in the newspaper. I wouldn't budge. The cotillion, a turning point for the upper-class girl, signaling her preparation for high society, was economically out of reach for the average black family, and I wanted no part of the whole scene. One of the frivolities of the elite, I thought. When I stood my ground, Grandma tried to elicit support from Mom and Dad. Since they did not have strong feelings either way, they left the decision up to me.

I was appreciative of the fact that my parents had not placed class restrictions on my friendships or preached

From three generations of Isum women: Zellee (l.) Rachel (c.), and Annetta Jones (r.), I learned the importance of defining life on your own terms (though their advice some- times back-fired!).

any stereotypes associated with one group of people over another. Instead, they reinforced values: education, service, achievement, and family. Their only restriction was a ban on public dances. Even their insistence on our membership in Jack & Jill (an exclusive social group for African-American families) was not about class so much as an attempt to balance the whiteness of our home and school environments. As the deadline for cotillion recommendations encroached, my grandmother made one final attempt to sway me. Again, I declined.

INTEGRITY

The Lion at Dusk

by Roger Kahn

My father's life is filled with examples of integrity. From his ten years as a Brooklyn Dodger, to his work with youth and the founding of Freedom National Bank, my father rarely backed down from what he believed in. But, at a press conference to announce his retirement from baseball, a sportswriter questioned his integrity and was quickly reminded of what Jackie Robinson stood for.

◆ ◆ ◆

EVEN ROBINSON'S DECLINING baseball years crackled with controversy. During Walter Alston's first spring as [Brooklyn Dodgers'] manager, he said in Vero Beach, "Every man on this ball club will have to fight for his job." Some veterans laughed. Duke Snider did not expect to spend the season of 1954 on the bench. Pee Wee Reese was offended. Jackie Robinson spoke out. "I don't know what the hell that man is trying to do. Upset us all?" That year a strong, mismanaged, discontented Dodger team finished second.

My dad brought an element of excitement to the game of baseball. He danced between bases, choosing the least suspected moment to steal from one base to another. His retirement announcement created the same kind of shock in the sports community.

In succeeding seasons the Dodgers won two pennants, but for Robinson the old spirit vanished. He felt out of things, he said. This manager was hostile. This front office did not provide support. Then, after the 1956 season, Walter O'Malley traded him to the Giants. "We hate to lose Jackie," O'Malley said, "but it is necessary for the good of the team."

To find similar cynicism, you had to go clear back to 1935 when the Yankees dumped Babe Ruth on the old Boston Braves. But then the star was being sent to another league. Robinson, the embodiment of the loud, brave, contentious Dodgers, was being assigned to his team's great adversary. Sports pages flapped with excitement. Robinson deserved it. O'Malley was outrageous. The Polo Grounds was no Valhalla.

Ed Fitzgerald, the editor of *Sport* magazine, commissioned an artist to paint a cover portrait in which Sal Maglie, who had come to Brooklyn early in 1956, stood at the mound, glowering at Giant base runner Jackie Robinson. "Maglie of the Dodgers against Robinson of the Giants," Fitzgerald said. "*Un*-believable. But would you first find out if Jackie's gonna play?"

Robinson was vague when I telephoned. The money was good, he said. The Giants were offering $40,000 for one year; then they'd pay him $20,000 for each of the next two seasons as a part–time scout.

"So you're going to accept?"

"You know me."

"Well, do you expect to play?"

"Whatever I do, I'll give it all I got."

What Robinson was trying to say (and has never known how to say) was "No comment." A month later on a chilly Sunday afternoon in January, *Look* magazine called "a press conference of major importance involving Dodger great Jackie Robinson."

At four o'clock in a wood-paneled conference room off Madison Avenue, *Look*'s promotion men distributed press releases and tearsheets of an article "copyright 1957, Cowles Magazines, Inc." Above Robinson's by-line, the story was headed: "Why I'm Quitting Baseball." Robinson explained that he was thirty-eight and had a family to support. He had been offered a job as vice president for personnel at Chock Full O'Nuts, a chain of lunch counters staffed almost entirely by Negroes. He was "to keep turnover at a minimum." "So," he wrote, "I'm through with baseball. From now on I'll be just another fan — a Brooklyn fan."

Reporters sat in overstuffed black-leather chairs and sipped Scotch. Their first questions were gentle. Help? Yes, Robinson conceded, he'd had help with the article. Had the Giant trade made him quit? No, he'd already begun working on the story when Buzzy Bavasi called him.

"Didn't you lie to your friends?" someone said suddenly.

"I did not lie."

"Mislead?"

Dan Mich, a large, square-faced man, stepped forward. "I run *Look,*" Mich said, in a presidential tone. "Any statement Jack made that may have been misleading was out of respect for us. I've never met anyone more honest." The conference descended to chatter and morning newspapermen left to make their deadlines.

Back home in Stamford that night, Robinson faced doubts that would not let down. He had said that he was quitting and he had meant that he was quitting, but a Giant executive called to propose a still better contract. If the offer improved further, Jack simply would have to change his mind. *Look,* Robinson reasoned, would be getting $50,000 worth of publicity. He was square there, he felt. Now it might be fun making Walter O'Malley look like a clown of a trader. Then two days later Buzzy Bavasi told reporters, "Robinson will play. I know the guy and he likes money. Now that *Look*'s paid him, he'll play so he can collect from the Giants, too."

Reading these sentences, Robinson knew: the retirement would have to be permanent. Already Red Smith was attacking him "for peddling a news story, the rights to his retirement." If he did play again, critics would denounce him as a phony. His baseball years, begun with heroic pioneering, could end amid cries of fraud. "Goddam, I can't play," Robinson told himself, cheerlessly, but the doubts endured until the first day of the 1957 season. That morning his right knee, crippled by a thousand slides, was so swollen he could not get out of bed. . . .

"I'll miss the excitement of baseball," Robinson wrote in *Look,* "but now I'll be able to spend more time with my family. My kids and I will get to know each other better. Jackie, Sharon and David will have a real father they can play with and talk to in the evening and every weekend. They won't have to look for him on TV."

"Maybe my sons will want to play ball, as I have, when they grow up. I'd love it if they do. But I'll see to it they get a college education first, and meet the kind of people who can help them later."

"Just now Jackie still feels badly about my quitting. It's tough for a ten-year-old to have his dad suddenly turn from a ball player into a commuter. I guess it will be quite a change for me, too. But someday Jackie will realize that the old man quit baseball just in time."

Old Men by the Fire

INTEGRITY

by David Remnick

Thirteen years after my father's first game in a Dodgers' uniform, another lone giant stepped forward and took a courageous stance that rocked the world far beyond the sport he excelled in. In 1960, Muhammad Ali beat Sonny Liston and became the heavyweight world champion. Two years later, in the midst of an escalating and controversial Vietnam War, he was ordered to an Army induction center. A reporter called Ali to ask him if he had any comment about his certain draft. Comment he did!

♦ ♦ ♦

THIS WAS A BIG STORY, evoking memories of other young athletes and pop stars drafted at the peak of their careers: Joe Louis, Ted Williams, Elvis Presley. But this was different, this was Vietnam, a far more ambiguous and confusing event. It was confusing, not least, to Muhammad Ali. By now he was accustomed to being asked about racial politics, but now he was hearing new questions: What do you think of LBJ? What's your

Muhammad Ali (born Cassius Clay) burst onto the international sports scene in 1960 when he won the Gold Medal at the Tokyo Olympics. A three-time world heavyweight boxing champion, Ali's reach extended far beyond the confines of the boxing ring.

view of the draft? What do you think about the war? What about the Vietcong? For a while, Ali stumbled.

"Then all of sudden he hit the note," [Bob] Lipsyte [*New York Times* reporter] remembered.

"Man," Ali finally told one reporter, "I ain't got no quarrel with them Vietcong. . . ."

In the coming days and months, Ali's phones rang incessantly, with calls not only from reporters, but from people who wanted to express their hatred, to tell him they hoped he'd die. But others called in their support, including the British philosopher and pacifist Bertrand Russell.

"In the coming months," Russell wrote to Ali later, "there is no doubt that the men who rule Washington will try to damage you in every way open to them, but I am sure you know that you spoke for your people and for the oppressed everywhere in the courageous defiance of American power. . . ."

At about the time Ali got Russell's letter, the government confiscated his passport. From then on, Ali took a fiercely political stand and went from one college campus to the next, speaking out against the war. He learned more about Vietnam and deepened his understanding of what was happening both to the country and to himself. He would not kill Vietnamese on behalf of a government that barely recognized the humanity of his own people. In the short term, the decision not to serve cost Ali everything: his title, his popularity among millions of people, and, undoubtedly, millions of dollars. . . .

As time passed and the government put pressure on him, Ali made his stance firmer, clearer. He would not fight exhibitions for the army. He would not move abroad. "Why should they ask me to put on a uniform and go ten thousand miles from home and drop bombs and bullets on brown people in Vietnam while so-called Negro people in Louisville are treated like dogs?" he said to a reporter for *Sports Illustrated*. "If I thought going to war would bring freedom and equality to twenty-two million of my people, they wouldn't have to draft me. I'd join tomorrow. But I either have to obey the laws of the land or the laws of Allah. I have nothing to lose by standing up and following my beliefs. We've been in jail for four hundred years."

On the morning of April 28, 1967, Ali appeared at the U.S. Armed Forces Examining and Entrance Station on San Jacinto Street in Houston, where he had been summoned to face induction. On the sidewalk, a group of protesters, mainly students but some older people, too, were already there chanting, "Don't go! Don't go!" "Draft beer — not Ali!" H. Rap Brown, one of the leading activists from the Student Nonviolent Coordinating Committee, was shouting, "Hep! Hep! Don't take that step!" Brown flashed Ali the raised fist, the black power sign, and Ali answered in kind. Then he went inside to face army induction.

"It's hard now to relay the emotion of that time," said Sonia Sanchez, the poet and civil rights activist. "This was still a time when hardly any well-known people were resisting the draft. It was a war that was disproportionately killing young black brothers, and here was this beautiful, funny, poetical young man standing up and saying no! Imagine it for a moment! The heavyweight champion, a magical man, taking his fight out of the ring and into the arena of politics, and standing firm. The message that sent!"

Ali and twenty-five other potential recruits were told to fill out papers, undergo physical examinations, and then wait for the long bus ride to Fort Polk, Louisiana. In the early afternoon, the recruits lined up in front of a young lieutenant, S. Steven Dunkley, for one last formality. The officer called each man's name and told him to take another step forward — and into the armed forces. Finally, Ali's name was called — "Cassius Clay! Army!" Ali did not move. He was called "Ali" and again he remained still. Then another officer led Ali to a private room and advised him that the penalty for refusing the draft was five years imprisonment and a fine. Did he understand? Yes, he did. Ali was given another chance to respond to his name and step forward. Again he stood still. There was no fear in

Ali, none of the anxiety he'd felt in those few minutes warming up in the ring before facing Liston for the first time. Finally, one of the induction officers told Ali to write out a statement with his reasons for refusal.

"I refuse to be inducted into the armed forces of the United States," Ali wrote, "because I claim to be exempt as a minister of the religion of Islam."

Ali stepped outside the building and into a hive of reporters. The protesters were still there, too, and shouted encouragement. But even years later, Ali also remembered a woman carrying a small American flag and shouting, "You're headin' straight for jail! You get down on your knees and beg forgiveness from God! My son's in Vietnam and you no better than he is. I hope you rot in jail."

Ali's refusal to go to Vietnam touched young people, especially young African-Americans, profoundly. Gerald Early, a professor of literature who has written deeply on the "culture of bruising," recalled that moment in 1967 in his essay "Tales of the Wonderboy": "When he refused, I felt something greater than pride: I felt as though my honor as a black boy had been defended, my honor as a human being. He was the grand knight, after all, the dragon-slayer. And I felt myself, little inner-city boy that I was, his apprentice to the grand imagination, the grand daring. The day that Ali refused the draft, I cried in my room. I cried for him and for myself, for my future and his, for all our black possibilities."

Ali was sentenced to five years in prison and a ten-thousand-dollar fine — the maximum. Eventually, in June 1971, the Supreme Court would vindicate him in a unanimous decision, but after knocking out Zora Folley one month after refusing the draft, he would not fight for three and a half years, the prime of his boxing life. He would not regain the heavyweight championship until 1974, when he outfoxed George Foreman on the ropes in Kinshasa, Zaire. "I figure that decision cost him ten million dollars in purses, endorsements, and the rest," said Gordon Davidson. It also cost him the goodwill of many Americans who thought that he was a rich young man in perfect health avoiding military service and using religion as an excuse. But Ali would never regret the price. He watched his old friend from Louisville, Jimmy Ellis, and then Joe Frazier, take his title. *His* title, which he had coveted from the time he was twelve. But even for a young man in love with his fame, there were greater priorities.

COURAGE DETERMINATION

TEAMWORK PERSISTENCE

INTEGRITY **CITIZENSHIP**

JUSTICE COMMITMENT

EXCELLENCE COURAGE

DETERMINATION TEAMWORK

PERSISTENCE INTEGRITY

CITIZENSHIP JUSTICE

COMMITMENT EXCELLENCE

EXCELLENCE COURAGE

DETERMINATION TEAMWORK

PERSISTENCE INTEGRITY

CITIZENSHIP Jazz and Activism

Over the years, the dinner conversation at our house revolved around baseball, politics, justice, business and banking, the Black Panther Party, the NAACP, Dr. Martin Luther King, Reverend Jesse Jackson, school desegregation, civil rights marches, fire hoses, the right to vote, along with homework, sports, dance classes, piano and bed. But, the night we learned that Dr. King was actually coming to our house we couldn't sleep for the anticipation of meeting our hero.

◆　◆　◆

ALL AROUND ME the temperatures were rising in the battle for civil rights. In 1963, my family, along with hundreds of thousands of others, traveled to the March on Washington. Early in the day I fainted from the extreme heat and massive crowds. Thankfully, I recovered in time to hear Dr. King.

That same summer my father spearheaded a New York fund-raising drive for the Southern Christian Leadership Conference. Several churches in the South had been bombed in protest against Dr. King's work.

In 1963, we hosted Dr. Martin Luther King, Jr. at our home in Stamford, Connecticut. My parents chose jazz as a way to bridge communities and raise dollars for the jailed civil rights workers. In 1971, my dad became a founding board member of Jesse Jackson's Operation PUSH and continued his commitment to social change.

Mom and Dad wanted to help. They decided to host a jazz concert on the lawn of our Stamford home to raise bail money for a fund Dr. King had established for the jailed civil rights activists.

My brothers and I swelled with excitement when we learned that Dr. Martin Luther King, Jr. would be coming to our home! We volunteered to help get the house and grounds ready. The day of the concert, friends arrived early with platters of fried chicken, salads, cakes, cookies, and brownies to add to the feast that my mother and grandmother had stayed up half the night preparing. Dad stayed on the phone right up to the last moment, working out the details with the performers and Dr. King's staff. Everything had to be perfect.

At the suggestion of sunrise, Mom roused the troops by blasting spirituals. Jackie, David, and I bathed and made our beds so that our rooms would be neat before the artists and guests arrived. It was a clear summer day and the tent that had been erected the day before sat in green-and-white-striped splendor at the base of the hill.

My parents opened our home, surrendered our grounds, and welcomed the public. Dad, determined that his lawn was going to survive this day, decided to take personal responsibility for directing the parking of the cars.

I was surprised that Dr. King's arrival was met without ceremony. He greeted my parents warmly and Dad made the formal introductions. We stood in mute witness, not sure what to say to this famous man. Ordinarily, I wasn't thrown by celebrities, but Dr. King was different. He had a deep, seductive Southern accent and standing in his presence was as close to God as I figured I would ever get.

The day proceeded smoothly. People came, the music flowed throughout the afternoon, and Dad said we made lots of money. Dr. King moved easily among the people sprawled on the lawn. As the day wound down, Dad and Dr. King thanked the people for coming and he made a quiet exit. While the details of the day remain fuzzy in my mind, the impact has lasted. We had been listening to our parents for years, learning about our history secondhand. This day was special because it made Jackie, David, and I active participants. No, we hadn't picketed or fought off dogs, like the kids in the South, but we had helped raise money to support an aspect of the movement.

But just as Dad's fame had ushered us into front-row seats on the steps of the Lincoln Memorial to hear Dr. King deliver his "I Have a Dream" speech that August day, so had it put us on the front line of so much that was happening nationwide. Seven years of retirement from baseball had not lessened that fact of our lives — it escalated it.

The same year as Dr. King's speech, Governor George Wallace literally made a federal case of keeping two black students from entering the University of Alabama as a huge battalion of soldiers in battle gear with rifles drawn stood in wait; Medgar Evers, the NAACP's crusader, was shot dead in the driveway of his home while local officials made a hero of his arrogant killer; days after the inspiring multiracial "high" of the March on Washington, reality killed four young girls when a pro-segregationist's bomb tore the roof off their Birmingham church; President Kennedy publicly mourned the girls, condemning the violence on national television, and within weeks personally joined the amazing list of hate's victims when he was killed in Dallas. Amazingly, all of this happened in six months — May to November 1963, as I completed junior high.

From The Hall of Fame to Birmingham

by Jackie Robinson

Citizenship can mean membership in a community or a commitment to service. In the following selection, my father talks about his personal commitment to serve the Civil Rights Movement. He also talks about the conflicting messages he received as an African-American citizen in a segregated, often racist society.

◆ ◆ ◆

BASEBALL IS ONLY A PASTIME, a sport, an entertainment, a way of blowing off steam. But it is also *the* national game, with an appeal to Americans of every race, color, creed, sex or political opinion. It unites Americans in the common cause of rooting for the home team.

Is it possible that Americans value victory for the home team more than the victory of democracy in our national life?

I ask this question in light of two contrasting experiences. In 1962 I was awarded baseball's highest honor, membership in the Hall of Fame. I was welcomed to

When we built our home in Stamford, Connecticut, Mom designated a room to show-case Dad's trophies and awards. I had my favorites like a sterling silver replica of a championship bat and Dad's bronzed football cleat from UCLA. Dad cherished his Baseball Hall of Fame plaque.

beautiful Cooperstown, New York, where the high officials of baseball did everything in their power to make that day the happiest of my life. No one mentioned that I was the first Negro in the Hall of Fame, or that another bastion of prejudice had fallen.

No one was thinking about such things that day. I was thinking that the effort and energy I had put into playing ball for [the] dear old Brooklyn [Dodgers] had been recognized, that my name and record now stood beside those of Babe Ruth, Ty Cobb, Joe DiMaggio and the other guys who'd also played to win — if you'll pardon both the comparison and the cliché. And that small boys, some of them Negro boys, would visit Cooperstown in the future and read my plaque and say, "Did you ever see Jackie Robinson steal home, Dad? Show me how he did it when we go home, will ya, Dad?"

That fall James Meredith tried to enroll in the University of Mississippi. The Civil War, which had apparently ended in 1865, broke out anew. Soon the battlefront spread from state to state, from South to North. In my ball-playing days I had been invited to become a life member of the National Association for the Advancement of Colored People (NAACP). The fee was $500 but I didn't know enough about the Association's aims to feel that I should contribute that sort of money to it.

But after I retired from baseball I learned what the NAACP was doing to improve the lot of Negroes throughout the United States. I joined up and am now co-chairman of the life membership recruiting drive. Now, suddenly, the NAACP and its allies are engaged in this new kind of war against prejudice, with as great a stake in freedom for our country as if we were being invaded by a foreign power.

I'd been in the first skirmishes of that democratic war, wearing a ball player's uniform. I was in it again, in 1963. With Floyd Patterson, Archie Moore, Curt Flood of the St. Louis Cardinals, and other Negroes of the sports entertainment fields I went to Jackson, Mississippi, in January. We went there to stiffen the morale of those who were suffering economic and political oppression from the "Know-Nothings" of Mississippi.

Our stay in Jackson was brief and uneventful. We attended a banquet, made speeches and departed, inspired by the courage of those on the front lines, one of whom was the soon-to-be martyred Medgar Evers.

In May the battle of Alabama began. Many warned me to avoid incurring the wrath of Bull Connor's police in Birmingham. Some people have asked why Floyd Patterson and I went there. We didn't have to go. We didn't go for what we personally might accomplish. [Brave men and women under the leadership of Dr. Martin Luther King had laid] the groundwork for resistance to rabid segregationists and the integration of Birmingham Negroes into the city's economic life. Floyd and I went to Birmingham to give our thanks to the fighting people who were standing fast against fire-hoses, police dogs, riot clubs, guns and bombs.

Remember this: Cooperstown, New York, and Birmingham, Alabama, are both in the United States. In Cooperstown I had been a guest of honor in the company of three other new Hall of Famers: Bill McKechnie, Edd Roush and Bob Feller. In Birmingham I was "that negrah who pokes his nose into other peoples' puddin'."

From the moment of our arrival Floyd and I were watched like criminals come to town to plan a bank robbery, like potential despoilers of Southern woman-hood.

We registered at the Gaston Motel in the Negro ghetto. We addressed a large assemblage in a Negro church. Our next destination was a second church where boys and girls waited to express their faith in the Birmingham fight for freedom. As we entered our car, state troopers blocked the driveway to prevent us from backing out. We waited until the police car moved away. As we started up the road, two other police cars came out of the night, forming a roadblock.

A young representative of the Southern Christian Leadership Conference was at the wheel. He hesitated.

Would we be arrested for making a U-turn? He took the chance and sped away in the opposite direction.

As he parked before the second church, a young man approached. "We saw what just happened," he said. "It won't happen here. There's strength in numbers. When you leave, fall in behind our cars and let them try to block us."

However, nothing out of the ordinary occurred and we drove back to the motel without incident.

The motel was a scene of destruction. It had been bombed a few days earlier. State and local police were massed outside, facing Negroes who were prepared to defend victims of fresh violence. Rumors were current that Klansmen were rallying in the city's outskirts.

The bomb had wrecked the dining room. Floyd and I had not eaten since our arrival in Birmingham, so we decided to look for a nearby restaurant. "There's one about two blocks away," we were told. "But you'd better be extremely careful. Don't speak to anyone on the street. The cops are hoping you'll start something, so they can pin a charge on you."

We looked neither to left nor to right as we walked the two blocks, a police car trailing us at the curb, parking before the little restaurant while we ate. Afterwards, it trailed us back to the motel.

The following morning Floyd and I paid our respects to the brother of Martin Luther King, the Reverend A.D. King, whose home had twice been bombed. The first bomb had been tossed on the lawn, twenty feet from the house. If it had hit its mark as the second bomb had, the dwelling would have been demolished, its occupants killed. . . .

"I saw five cops standing on a poor woman," another young man told me. "They picked her up, tossed her into the truck and took her off to jail. . . ."

These horrors happened in the United States on the day Giants fans were cheering Willie Mays' two home runs and Dodger fans were shouting themselves hoarse after Tommy Davis' game-saving one-hand grab of a 400-foot wallop.

In Birmingham Negroes were saying, "If we gotta die we may as well take someone with us!" In ballparks whites were yelling, "We're with you, Willie! We're with you, Tommy! Attaboy!"

CITIZENSHIP

Parents As Mentors

by Marian Wright Edelman

When I think about citizenship, I think about community service. That's why I have selected an essay by Marian Wright Edelman. As a lifetime advocate for women and children, her sense of civic commitment was learned in her childhood. Her story reminds me of the gentle indoctrination into a lifetime of service my brothers and I received from our parents.

◆　◆　◆

MY BELIEF THAT I AND OTHERS could do more than complain, wring hands, or give in to despair at the wrongs rife in the world stem from my parents' examples. Daddy, a teacher-preacher who never raised his voice in the pulpit and who tried to educate our congregation's mind as well as touch its heart, taught that faith required action and that action could be sustained only by faith in the face of daily discouragement and injustice in our segregated southern society. Because the public playgrounds and many public services were closed

DEAR LORD
BE GOOD TOME
THE SEA IS SO
WIDE AND
MY BOAT IS
SO SMALL

ildren fen

Marian Wright Edelman is a lawyer, activist, advocate, author, and founder and president of the Children's Defense Fund. Because of her nearly thirty years championing the rights of children, she ranks high among my list of sheroes.

to Black children, Mama and Daddy made our church a hub for children. Boy and Girl Scout troops, boxing, skating, ball games, and other physical activities provided outlets for pent-up boys' and girls' energy. Choirs, children's days, pageants, and vacation Bible school made church a welcoming haven rather than a boring chore. And the great preachers and role models invited to speak at Shiloh helped challenge our minds and widen our horizons and remind us of the sky above and of the rainbows in the clouds.

My outrage about children who die needlessly from preventable diseases and curable sickness today is a result of my parents' sadness over the senseless death of little Johnny Harrington, who lived three doors down from our church parsonage and did not get a tetanus shot after stepping on a nail. His good and hard-working grandmother didn't have the money or the knowledge to take him to the emergency room and nobody acted until it was too late.

My concern for safe places for children to play and swim comes from the lack of public playgrounds for Black children when I was growing up and our exclusion from the swimming pool near my home where I could see and hear White children splashing happily. A childhood friend died when he jumped off the bridge into the shallow hospital-sewage-infected waters of Crooked Creek near my home and broke his neck.

And I almost drowned in a segregated public lake in Cheraw, South Carolina that lacked adequate lifeguard surveillance. Daddy and Mama built a playground behind our church with a skating rink and swings and sliding boards and lights so children could play at night and Mama opened a canteen with sodas and snacks so that young people could have someplace safe and fun to go.

My advocacy for equitable health care for all and outrage that our rich nation denies it to millions comes from the horror Daddy and I felt when we witnessed a White ambulance driver arrive on the scene of a middle-of-the-night collision near our home only to drive away, leaving behind seriously injured Black migrant workers after he saw that the White truck driver with whom they had collided was unhurt.

Daddy died on May 6, 1954 — eleven days before the U.S. Supreme Court's *Brown v. Board of Education* decision that he had waited and watched for. My mother carried on our family's rituals and responsibilities valiantly — doing what she had to do to continue preparing us for life.

My concern for children without homes and parents unable to care for them comes from the foster children my mother took into our home after Daddy died. I am still ashamed of my resentment and jealousy when I was asked to share my room with a homeless child for a few days. As I grew older, nearly a dozen foster sisters and brothers were reared by my mother.

An elderly White man asked me what I did for a living when I was home for my mother's funeral in 1984. I realized and told him I do, perhaps on a larger scale, exactly what my parents did: serve and advocate for children and the poor.

COURAGE DETERMINATION

TEAMWORK PERSISTENCE

INTEGRITY CITIZENSHIP

JUSTICE COMMITMENT

EXCELLENCE COURAGE

DETERMINATION TEAMWORK

PERSISTENCE INTEGRITY

CITIZENSHIP JUSTICE

COMMITMENT EXCELLENCE

EXCELLENCE COURAGE

DETERMINATION TEAMWORK

PERSISTENCE INTEGRITY

Turned My Wailing Into Dancing

After compiling an initial list of nine values to be celebrated in the
Breaking Barriers *program, I discussed the list with my mother.*
We agreed that all but one principle applied to my father's life. That
principle was tolerance. Mom asked me if I would want to be toler-
ated. I took offense at the suggestion and immediately got her point.
In the end, we substituted justice for tolerance avoiding the passiv-
ity inherent in "to be tolerated."

My dad believed strongly in treating all people fairly and
equally. In the later part of his life, he took his fight for justice a step
further by serving on Connecticut's judicial appeals board.

Dad used every opportunity he was given to point out the in-
justices around us. The 1972 World Series was an excellent exam-
ple. Major League Baseball took this jewel event to honor my father
and he refused to back down. Instead of simply accepting his mo-
ment of glory, Dad spoke out against the injustice that remains in
professional sports. I was thrilled to be a witness to what turned out
to be my father's final public appearance.

◆　◆　◆

During the 1972 World Series game in Cincinnati, Major League Baseball celebrated my father's 25th anniversary of breaking the color barrier. We were so proud of my father for using this event to remind the world that equality and justice was still the goal.

THE NEXT WEEKEND I was on a flight that took less than two hours. I arrived in Cincinnati before my family, checked for their arrival gate, and hurried to meet them.

I spotted David first. Walking next to him was a woman I didn't recognize, but I was struck by her statuesque appearance. Must be Tish, David's new model girlfriend I'd heard about but hadn't met. It was strange seeing my bohemian brother's six-foot slender body clad in a gray suit and an obviously new pair of black dress shoes. David had seemingly traded his contempt for the trappings of the middle class and joined forces with the majority. Since his return from Africa, David had been driving Dad from our home in Stamford into Manhattan each day for work. This arrangement had stopped recently when David accepted a job writing for an independent film company based in Manhattan. My parents had hired a driver to take his place.

Dad's five-foot-eleven-inch, two-hundred-and-twenty-five pound frame was stooped slightly. His long arms swung at his sides as he tried to maintain a steady gait. Mom and Dad were still a handsome couple though, and Mom looked stunning. Through sheer determination, she had maintained her size-ten figure and started wearing her mixed black and silver hair naturally. Her mocha chocolate complexion was flawless.

At breakfast the next morning David arrived in his gray suit once again. Dad teased David, with a mixture of joy and pride, about his one and only outfit. At each opportunity, Dad introduced Tish as David's fiancé. I now understand that my father was feeling the relief of living to see his youngest child become an adult.

As the World Series got under way the following afternoon, we laughed and cheered for both teams. The sun kept the October chill at bay. All day long people came by to greet Dad and he proudly introduced his family. Of all the stars on the field Dad was undeniably the hero, and it was clearly his day.

Although there had been many opportunities before for David and me to hear Dad tell the story of his early years in baseball, this was a day designed for memories. David, Tish, and I literally sat on the edge of our seats directly behind Mom and Dad asking question after question. I tried to envision the highly emotional and potentially volatile stands with their eyes on Number 42.

"Dad, if this was one of the segregated ballparks, where would the Jim Crow section be?" I asked. My eyes followed Dad's hand as he pointed toward the out-field section.

"The area would be so crowded that the fans would fill every square inch," Dad replied. "I never was quite sure if they didn't have enough seats or were just too excited to sit down," Dad added with a laugh. He told us how a cheer went up from the Jim Crow section at the smallest of his movement, like when he bent to tie his shoes.

"Weren't you too nervous to play?" David wanted to know.

"At times," Dad replied with a wistful look.

"Were you lonely?" I asked tentatively, fearful of his answer.

"Lonely . . . I had your mother in the stands and by my side each moment. That helped."

Dad fielded the questions with pride, not holding back the frustration at the lack of progress some twenty-five years later. He talked more of the mission than of the glory of the moment. He said he knew from the start that there was no quitting.

David and I absorbed every word silently, wishing that we had been there. I thought of some of the phrases used to describe Dad's finesse on the baseball diamond — the fire, the strategist, and the multiple threat. People referred to his having been blessed with speed and coordination. They said that he seemed at his best when the pressure was the greatest and that the part of baseball he loved the most was running the bases.

Halfway through the game a representative from Major League Baseball came to get us. We had to walk a distance to get to the entrance to the field. The chatter stopped. An air of seriousness took over. Dad hadn't shared his remarks with us, but he gave the impression of a man on a mission.

As Dad was introduced a roar went up from the fans. I looked around but I couldn't see faces. Movement — yes. Voices — loudly. But expressions were lost. David, Tish, and I stood facing Mom and Dad. I fought back tears. Dad was squinting. I guess he, too, was trying to make out faces. Plaques were exchanged. A telegram was read from President Nixon, who apologized for not being able to attend the ceremonies. And to think we almost didn't come because we didn't want to appear to be supporting Nixon's reelection. I couldn't resist exchanging a smirk with David.

Finally, Dad took the microphone. It was hard to accept the fact that this man whom I loved so dearly was becoming more disabled each day. I watched him as he winced in pain, and stepped forward, barely able to see five feet in front of him.

Photographers, TV cameras, reporters, were everywhere. Millions of Americans were watching and listening. Dad made the appropriate introductions and thanked all those involved, cleared his throat, looked out into the stands, almost as if he could see those faces, and said: "When I look down the third baseline, I want to see a black man coaching. Then I'll be able to say we've made progress."

That's all the press needed. Cameras flicked a mile a

minute. The outspoken, controversial Jackie Robinson had done it again. On his day of glory, he had come to make a final statement to baseball and the world. He challenged them once again to take the leadership and integrate the ranks of management as they did the playing field some twenty-five years earlier. David and I exchanged smiles. We were especially proud of our father on this day.

◆　◆　◆

Imagine if my father and the many other ballplayers of color who followed him hadn't been given the opportunity to showcase their talents on a Major League Baseball field. The world of professional sports wouldn't hold the same glamour, excitement, and success that it now has. More importantly, the men and women who play in team sports wouldn't have learned the benefits of living in a just society. Now, this is not to say that we've achieved full justice yet in sports, or in life. But, the achievements of my father, and other people like him, remind us of what's possible and help us keep the pressure on toward a just and equal world

As a Major League ballplayer, my father learned a compelling lesson that haunted him well into his final days. As the struggle for justice and equality continues, we as a people and a strong nation can not afford to forget that lesson, either.

I Never Had It Made

by Jackie Robinson

While my father's exit from baseball stirred controversy, he made a timely decision. Just as opportunities opened up for him in the business and political communities, the Civil Rights Movement was heating up and Dad wanted to be a part of it. It was an exciting and challenging time to be an activist. Years later, my father summed up his life in his autobiography, explaining why he insisted on the title: I Never Had It Made.

♦   ♦   ♦

LIFE, IN SPITE OF ALL the ups and downs, has been very good to me individually. Personally I have been very fortunate. Why then, do I insist that my autobiography be titled "I Never Had It Made"?

It is because I refuse to kid myself about the value of having a comfortable home, about having a little money in the bank, about having received awards and trophies and honors and having had the opportunity to talk and work with some of the most influential people in the world in all phases of activity.

I'm thankful that my father's quest for justice didn't end when he retired from baseball. He lent his support to the Civil Rights Movement and the increasingly heated protests and freedom marches to end Jim Crow, or segregation, laws in this country.

A life is not important except in the impact it has on other lives.

Everything I ever got I fought hard for — and Rachel fought by my side — but I know that I haven't got the right to say truthfully that I have it made. I cannot possibly believe I have it made while so many of my black brothers and sisters are hungry, inadequately housed, insufficiently clothed, denied their dignity as they live in slums or barely exist on welfare. I cannot say I have it made while our country drives full speed ahead to deep rifts between men and women of varying colors, speeds along a course toward more and more racism.

Life owes me nothing. Baseball owes me nothing. But I cannot, as an individual, rejoice in the good things I have been permitted to work for and learn while the humblest of my brothers is down in a deep hole hollering for help and not being heard.

That is why I have devoted and dedicated my life to service. I don't like to be in debt. And I owe. Some of my friends tell me I've paid the note a thousandfold. But I still feel I owe — till every man can rent and lease and buy according to his money and his desires; until every child can have an equal opportunity in youth and manhood; until hunger is not only immoral but illegal; until hatred is recognized as a disease, a scourge, an epidemic, and treated as such; until racism and sexism and narcotics are conquered and until every man can vote and any man can be elected if he qualifies — until that day Jackie Robinson and no one else can say he has it made.

A Testament of Hope

by Dr. Martin Luther King, Jr.

My father's powerful entry into professional sports was an early step toward breaking down the walls of segregation in the United States. His success also helped promote a sense of African-American pride and helped generate a rising up of his people. Within this climate, leaders such as Dr. Martin Luther King, Jr. carried the mantle and led the way toward the struggle for justice and equality for all citizens.

Dr. King's influence spread far beyond the Civil Rights battlefield. His eloquence and his commitment to justice reaches deeply into our souls. Rereading Dr. King's A Testament of Hope, *I am struck by how his words apply as much as today they did twenty years ago. What I love most about this next passage is Dr. King's optimism and belief that a just society is attainable.*

◆　◆　◆

Whenever I am asked my opinion of the current state of the civil rights movement, I am forced to pause; it is not easy to describe a crisis so profound that it has caused the most powerful nation in the world to stagger in confusion and bewilderment. Today's problems

Whether you think of Dr. Martin Luther King as a freedom fighter or a savior, he was undeniably a man who met the challenges presented to him and in doing so changed the course of history.

are so acute because the tragic evasions and defaults of several centuries have accumulated to disaster proportions. The luxury of a leisurely approach to urgent solutions — the ease of gradualism — was forfeited by ignoring the issues for too long. The nation waited until the black man was explosive with fury before stirring itself even to partial concern. Confronted now with the interrelated problems of war, inflation, urban decay, white backlash and a climate of violence, it is now *forced* to address itself to race relations and poverty, and it is tragically unprepared. What might once have been a series of separate problems now merge into a social crisis of almost stupefying complexity.

I am not sad that black Americans are rebelling; this was not only inevitable but eminently desirable. Without this magnificent ferment among Negroes, the old evasions and procrastinations would have continued indefinitely. Black men have slammed the door shut on a past of deadening passivity. Except for the Reconstruction years, they have never in their long history on American soil struggled with such creativity and courage for their freedom. These are our bright years of emergence; though they are painful ones, they cannot be avoided. . . .

These words may have an unexpectedly optimistic ring at a time when pessimism is the prevailing mood. People are often surprised to learn that I am an optimist. They know how often I have been jailed, how frequently the days and nights have been filled with frustration and sorrow, how bitter and dangerous are my adversaries. They expect these experiences to harden me into a grim and desperate man. They fail, however, to perceive the sense of affirmation generated by the challenge of embracing struggle and surmounting obstacles. They have no comprehension of the strength that comes from faith in God and man. It is possible for me to falter, but I am profoundly secure in my knowledge that God loves us; he has not worked out a design for our failure. Man has the capacity to do right as well as wrong, and his history is a path upward, not downward. The past is strewn with the ruins of the empires of tyranny, and each is a monument not merely to man's blunders but to his capacity to overcome them. While it is a bitter fact that in America in 1968, I am denied equality solely because I am black, yet I am not a chattel slave. Millions of people have fought thousands of battles to enlarge my freedom; restricted as it still is, progress has been made. This is why I remain an optimist, though I am also a realist, about the barriers before us. Why is the issue of equality still so far from solution in America, a nation that professes itself to be democratic, inventive, hospitable to new ideas, rich, productive and awesomely powerful? The problem is so tenacious because, despite its virtues and attributes,

America is deeply racist and its democracy is flawed both economically and socially. All too many Americans believe justice will unfold painlessly or that its absence for black people will be tolerated tranquilly.

Justice for black people will not flow into society merely from court decisions nor from fountains of political oratory. Nor will a few token changes quell all the tempestuous yearnings of millions of disadvantaged black people. White America must recognize that justice for black people cannot be achieved without radical changes in the structure of our society. The comfortable, the entrenched, the privileged cannot continue to tremble at the prospect of change in the status quo.

COURAGE DETERMINATION

TEAMWORK PERSISTENCE

INTEGRITY CITIZENSHIP

JUSTICE **COMMITMENT**

EXCELLENCE COURAGE

DETERMINATION TEAMWORK

PERSISTENCE INTEGRITY

CITIZENSHIP JUSTICE

COMMITMENT EXCELLENCE

EXCELLENCE COURAGE

DETERMINATION TEAMWORK

PERSISTENCE INTEGRITY

COMMITMENT A Father's Love

IT WAS HIS [my dad's] official job to test the ice on the lake to determine its safety. It involved an elaborate ceremony, but we always took great delight when he announced that the ice, was, indeed, safe.

But before this could happen we had to get him out of the house, no easy feat. [My brother] David and I scrambled to help him find his gloves, hat, and coat. Then we sat impatiently waiting for him to put on his oversized black rubber boots. The wait was torture. When Dad was properly dressed for the frigid weather, he led the way carrying his equipment — a shovel and broomstick. We followed him through the living room, out the sliding glass doors, down the back stairs, and down the hill.

As we reached the edge of the lake, Dad proclaimed to the troops hot on his heels, "That's as far as you go." [My brothers] Jackie, David, [our friends] Willie, Christy, and I came to an abrupt halt. We lined up along the shoreline, and shouted words of encour-

Several times a year Dad would pack us into the car and we'd head to Grossinger's, a resort nestled in the Catskill Mountains. My brothers and I used the time to fine-tune our inherited athletic ability. As you can see a young fan joined us for a photo.

agement as Dad proceeded out onto the snow-covered ice.

The lake, which ran the length of our property and then continued for about an eighth of a mile down the road, was a source of great pleasure. . . . In summer we swam, fished, and rowed the boat to the shallow sand-banks and captured sunbathing turtles. In winter, the lake was reserved for figure skating and ice hockey.

Dad cleared the snow from his path with each measured step. Before he placed one big foot in front of the other, he would tap the ice with his broomstick. From the cleared spot he was able to estimate the depth of ice beneath his body. After what seemed like forever, Dad would reach the deepest part of the lake, give one last tap with his stick, then turn to us and call out: "Go get your skates!"

We would cheer as loudly as we could and race back up the hill to get our skates and shovels, since clearing the snow off the ice was a big part of the production. But it wouldn't be long before the boys' hockey sticks were battling the black rubber puck, while Christy and I were forming figure eights at the other end of the lake and Dad had made his way back to the house.

But sometimes Dad tapping would cause an air bubble to become dislodged. Then a loud rumble would roll across the lake and we would cry out in near hysterics for fear that the lake would open up and swallow Dad. Of course, it never did. But, given the remote possibility, I thought Dad was very brave.

Now I think it even more. He was as brave then as when he entered baseball, a feat it took me years to appreciate. It dawned on me only gradually what it had meant for him to break the baseball color line, the courage it took for him to enter uncharted, and dangerous, waters.

No one really knew what would happen. He had to feel his way along an uncleared path like a blind man tapping for clues. That was Jackie Robinson. And that was my dad — big, heavy, out there alone on the lake, tapping his way along so that the ice would be safe for us.

And he couldn't swim.

COMMITMENT

Jackie's Prison

by Jackie Robinson

Parents want to protect their children. Unfortunately, this is not always possible, especially during the teenage years. In our house, as my brothers and I moved from childhood to adolescence, our struggle for self-definition intensified. The decisions we made during this critical juncture in our lives had lifelong impact. After years of testing the ice for the rest of us, my brother Jackie stepped out and made a series of wrong decisions that ultimately led to his arrest. In spite of my parents' pain, they remained active and committed to seeing Jackie through this terrible period in his life. As a result, we as a family grew closer and began to communicate better.

◆ ◆ ◆

EVERY MOMENT OF AGONY we had ever suffered, every fear we had ever experienced, seemed worthwhile on one special day — after Jackie had spent a year in the Daytop [drug rehabilitation] program. That was the day that Kenny Williams [Daytop Director] told us confidentially that he believed our son was out of danger,

The burden of being Jack Roosevelt Robinson, Jr. was often too much for my brother to face. The fact that I adored him only made his often troubled life all the more difficult to observe.

that he was cured. He didn't tell Jackie this and he cautioned us against false hopes. It was necessary that vigilance continue to be observed to insure that Jackie did not backslide, as so many do; the fear that an ex-addict will revert to his old habits is genuine. One or two or, sometimes, ten years cannot guarantee that an ex-addict will not be driven back to addiction by weakness or by circumstance. Experts have found, however, that one of the most successful ways a former addict can keep himself cured is through deep involvement in helping others who are fighting addiction. Knowledge of this fact, added to his tremendous gratitude to his Daytop associates, made Jackie decide to become a member of the Daytop staff. He worked at the same Daytop house where he had been helped and did group work on the outside. He gave talks at schools, to young people's groups, to social clubs, and to church groups. He also conducted a rehabilitation group. We attended some of his activities and felt extremely proud of his development. After Jackie's death we learned from others whose lives he touched how much of an impact he had been having. He had been clean for three years, and he spoke with authority about all that he had been through — about the way he had become an addict, the reasons for it, the hell into which he had been plunged as an addict — stealing, robbing, pushing dope, pimping — anything to get the money for dope. He had learned at

Daytop that the core of the cure was in being absolutely and utterly honest with himself and with others. As a result, when he appeared before audiences, he didn't spare himself. He was merciless in laying his own soul bare, and because he was willing to be open about it, he had a conviction and a sincerity which had a powerful effect on those who heard him talk. Jackie, who had learned to love himself properly, was now able to love others adequately. His capacity for loving had opened up.

Rachel and I had been trying to think of ways to show our appreciation to the Daytop staff. One day, on a holiday late in May, we invited all the members of the Daytop family, perhaps about fifty of them, to a picnic on the grounds surrounding our house in Stamford. They arrived about ten in the morning. Seldom have I seen a more organized group. They had a kitchen crew which went to work and prepared some great salads. They had brought along chickens, watermelons, and other fruits to add to the food we were providing. They had work squads assigned to take care of every detail. Some of those who didn't have an assignment for the moment were out on the grounds playing ball.

We were delighted seeing Jackie's pride in his friends and sensing how much our warmth towards them and their warmth towards us meant to him. He was like a mother hen, supervising the whole affair —

the preparation of the food, the games, the cleaning up they did at the end of the day. About four thirty in the afternoon, they were ready to return to Daytop, and all of them came to Rachel and me saying what a fabulous time they had had, some of them declaring it was the greatest day of their lives. As that line of kids dwindled down, our son Jackie was the last. There was a proud look on his face that put a lump in my throat because I remembered. . . .

When Jackie had left home to go into the service. We drove him to the train and I suppose I had the thoughts any father has watching his son leave for service. I was proud of him and I was concerned because I knew quite well there was a chance he might never come back. I was worried because I knew that telling him good-bye was rough for Rachel. As he was about to leave us, Rachel reached out and took him in her arms in a loving hug. Impulsively, I wanted to do the same thing. But just as I raised my arms to embrace him, his hand shot up and stopped me, and he took my hand in his in a firm handclasp. In our unspoken language, I knew that the love was there but what he was telling me was that men don't embrace. And I understood. That had been several years ago. . . .

Now on the lawn of our home, on the evening of the picnic, our confused and lost kid who had gone off to war, who had experienced as much life in a few short and turbulent years as many never do in a life-time, that same kid had now become a young man, growing in self-esteem, growing in confidence, learning about life, and learning about the massive power of love. He stood in front of us, the last on that line of thankful guests, and reached out and grabbed Rachel and hugged her to him. I stuck out my hand to shake his hand, remembering the day of his departure for the service. He brushed my hand aside, pulled me to him, and embraced me in a tight hug.

That single moment paid for every bit of sacrifice, every bit of anguish, I had ever undergone.

I had my son back.

◆　◆　◆

We lost my brother Jackie when he was twenty-four. He died in a car accident on June 17, 1971. At the funeral, my brother David read a poem that he'd written for Jackie called "The Baptism." The poem ended with the words, "and, he was free." Cries erupted from every pew in the church.

I struggled with this concept, wanting desperately to believe that my brother was finally free and at peace. I watched my parents over the next few months, needing to understand how we all would go on. They walked slower, rarely smiled broadly, but still they got up each morning and went to work. I followed my parents lead; I, too, became resilient.

COMMITMENT

Making It Home

by Rachel Robinson

IN THE LAST YEARS of his life, Jack finally found the business opportunity he had been searching for since leaving baseball a decade earlier. Backed by a small group of investors organized by his lawyer and loyal friend, Marty Edelman, Jack established the Jackie Robinson Construction Company to build housing for families with low and moderate incomes. It was a prospect that shored up his failing health and fueled his courageous heart. . . .

Jack set up an office in Fort Lee, New Jersey, near that of one of the company's investors, Richard Cohen (the other investor was Mickey Weissman). His support group included Merlyn White, his strong executive assistant; Kiah Sayles, his aide-de-camp; and Joel Halpern, the owner of Halpern Building Corp. They surrounded him with skilled help and personal loyalty that knew no bounds. They were his final blessing. Marty was extraordinarily supportive and vigilant, and his devotion helped sustain Jack's will to achieve and capacity

My parents shared an enviable partnership, one that saw them through their personal and professional triumphs and tribulations.

to function. Each night at about 10 P.M. Marty would call Jack to review the day's events and make plans. I felt the calls were a tender way for a friend to ease his mentor into a quiet night of rest, and though I didn't know Marty at the time, I loved him for it.

Jack had a mild heart attack in 1968, and then another in 1970. His eyesight was failing, and he silently endured extreme pain in his legs. The new business helped Jack's morale immensely, but it could not prevent physical deterioration. And yet he kept going at his usual relentless pace. On one day in September 1971, for example, Jack played nine holes in a charity golf tournament in Westchester County, New York, taking time after play had finished to kibitz with spectators in the gallery. Then, after gathering up several sandwiches, we hopped in the car and drove five hours to Washington, D.C., to be in attendance as Sharon received her nurse's cap at Howard University. We were both so proud. This was important to our daughter, and Jack's love for her would not let him think of missing it. He was extremely tired, but he stayed after the ceremony to sign autographs for Sharon's classmates who surrounded him. This was the way Jack had always lived his life. We didn't talk about the shadow hovering over us, we maintained our individual schedules as best we could, and we squeezed in doctor's visits as necessary. It was like being in a race . . . a race with death.

One evening in early 1972, Jack arrived home visibly shaken. He had almost hit a car on the parkway: The near-miss forced him to finally admit that he had completely lost all peripheral vision. I immediately hired a chauffeur. But Jack, to show his disdain for the arrangement, rode up front with the driver and loudly played the all-news radio station WINS from Stamford to Fort Lee and back to curtail any attempts at conversation. Given his lifelong passion to be self-sufficient and his love of driving, his need for a chauffeur was an unmistakable indication of his growing dependency on others, and he hated it. When he grumbled about his driver, I just smiled to myself. I was relieved that he wasn't driving — and that I wasn't the chauffeur.

In the summer of 1972 it occurred to me that I should assemble the family to take a trip with Jack. You might call it a premonition. So, our old friend Marion Logan, my mother, Sharon, David, Jack, and I went to a lovely condo in Dragon's Bay, Jamaica, for a week. Through the years Jamaica had been our favorite place to be. Marty secured the location and made all of the arrangements. We had an excellent cook and housekeepers so we were totally free to live on the beach. Beaches in general held little attraction for Jack, but we persuaded him that the seawater would be good for his legs. How grateful I am for that trip. It gave us time together in close quarters to begin to heal from the loss of Jackie and to strengthen the bonds between us. David, who had dropped out of Stanford University after Jackie's death and was working in New York, had become a source of strength for Jack, going to meetings with him and generally giving his father someone acceptable to lean on. In Jamaica David acted as Jack's aide and protector on trips to and from the beach. Sharon, who adored her father and had been in Washington at Howard University, had time to be closer. In the evenings we played games and talked quietly in pairs. The week was a gift.

Our family gathered one other time, on October 15, 1972, when Jack was honored before the start of the second game of the World Series between the Reds and the Pirates at Riverfront Stadium, Cincinnati. When *Sepia* magazine asked all of us to pose for a formal family picture, Jack murmured, "the last hurrah." I winced. At the game he was seated with Commissioner Bowie Kuhn, sportswriter Joe Reichler, Peter O'Malley, Joe Black, and Larry Doby and was surrounded by his former teammates and opponents. The game of life was almost over for Jack, but he had his final say as he accepted the honors of the day. In a voice quavering with emotion, he said, "I'd like to live to see a black manager, I'd like to live to see the day when there is a black man coaching at third base." At the airport on the way home he seemed especially weary. I wondered if he felt his farewell statement to baseball had fallen on deaf ears. Old soldiers never never ever give up.

On October 22, 1972, while we were watching a football game together on television, Jack suddenly got up and turned the TV off, saying he had detected a flash in his good eye. Such bright flashes often signaled the rupture of a small blood vessel in the eye. A sickening thought raced between us. Without discussion, we called his doctor and scheduled an early-morning appointment. The devastating prognosis of blindness lingered in the air that night as we fell asleep in a tight embrace. Early the next morning, I was in the kitchen preparing breakfast, and Jack was dressing for the 9 A.M. appointment in New York. I looked up and Jack was rushing down the hallway from the bedroom to the kitchen, obviously headed for me. So I ran to him. He put his arms around me, said, "I love you," and just dropped to the floor.

As I swiftly moved to deal with the emergency, I had a vague feeling that in a fantasy of "what would I do if. . . ," I had rehearsed for this moment more than once. As I did what I could, I struggled to stay out of the mental abyss I sensed overcoming me, until help arrived. Our neighbor and friend Sidney Kweskin arrived, and then and only then did I cry and cry. My dearest Jack, my giant, had been struck down, striving to live and loving to the very end.

Within a few weeks, I conjured up a thought that never mitigated the sense of loss, but had only to do with my protective feeling: He made it home . . . safe.

COURAGE DETERMINATION

TEAMWORK PERSISTENCE

INTEGRITY CITIZENSHIP

JUSTICE COMMITMENT

EXCELLENCE COURAGE

DETERMINATION TEAMWORK

PERSISTENCE INTEGRITY

CITIZENSHIP JUSTICE

COMMITMENT EXCELLENCE

EXCELLENCE COURAGE

DETERMINATION TEAMWORK

PERSISTENCE INTEGRITY

A Grand Tribute

ON APRIL 15, 1997, 54,000 people crowded into the New York Mets' Shea Stadium to pay tribute to my dad. But, there were more than baseball fans in attendance that chilly spring night. President Clinton and an entourage of politicians flew in on *Air Force One.* Mets owners Fred Wilpon and Nelson Doubleday hosted Baseball Commissioner Bud Selig, Leonard Coleman, Reggie Jackson, and my dad's former teammates Joe Black and Ralph Branca, in their box. The politicians cut deals and enjoyed the game and ceremonies from a separate box.

Surrounded by dignitaries, some of whom were also friends, my family basked in the glow. We had a private moment with President Clinton before the press was ushered in for photos. My son, Jesse, a high school senior and All-American football star, was granted the awesome honor of throwing out the first ceremonial pitch. My mother greeted the fans and television audience with her usual grace, strength, and thoughtful comments.

April 15, 1997, Major League Baseball held the Mets game after the fifth inning for a ceremony in honor of the 50th anniversary of my dad breaking the color barrier. It was an awesome night!

The evening was a difficult one for me. The strong emotions that the tribute evoked competed with a state of pure exhaustion as my various worlds collided. I was a nurse–midwife back then and had stayed up the night before with a woman in labor. By the time the baseball tribute rolled around, I had gone forty-eight hours with no sleep. Lack of sleep wasn't my only worry, I fretted over everything: Would my six-foot-three athletic son throw a strike? Would my mother be able to read from her cue cards or should she try to memorize her comments? How would the tradition-minded fans react to the announcement of the retirement of the number 42, my father's Dodger number, throughout baseball?

After the fifth inning, President Clinton, using walking canes because of a knee injury, Bud Selig, and my mother walked out onto the field for a formal ceremony.

Bud opened the program with his announcement that Major League Baseball would retire Robinson's number 42 in perpetuity. "Number 42 belongs to Jackie Robinson for the ages," he said as the fans leaped to their feet with thunderous applause and a deafening roar of approval. Bud stepped aside as President Clinton stepped to the microphones.

"It's hard to believe that it was fifty years ago that a twenty-eight-year-old rookie changed the face of baseball and the face of America forever," the President said. "Jackie Robinson scored the go-ahead run that day; we've all been trying to catch up ever since." The crowd cheered wildly. After they finally calmed down, Clinton continued, calling for more progress toward racial equality and challenging the boardrooms of baseball and business to step up to the plate. "If Jackie Robinson were here today," President Clinton said, "he would say we have done a lot of good in the last fifty years, but we could do a lot better." Then he introduced my mother, Rachel. The fans clapped enthusiastically.

As my mother began to speak I thought of the ancient Japanese saying, which hangs in her kitchen: *Now that my house has burned to the ground, I have a better view of the moon.* To the fans she was Mrs. Jackie Robinson. To us, she is the mother of two living children, the grandmother of nine, great grandmother of one, and surrogate mother to hundreds of Jackie Robinson scholars and alumnae.

I watched proudly from the suite, my arm locked around the waist of my friend, Santita Jackson, as the matriarch of our family delivered her speech. "I believe the greatest tribute we can pay to Jackie Robinson is to gain new support for a more equitable society," my mother said, "and in this heady environment of unity it is my hope that we can carry this living legacy beyond this glorious moment."

It *was* a glorious, proud moment, not just for my family, but for the millions of people who respected my dad and saw in his victory hope for the future.

And hope is the balm that keeps us striving for excellence.

Michael Jordan

by *Bob Greene*

"MY OWN HERO?" Jordan said. "I've never really had one."

He was so accustomed to being considered a hero to other people that I had wondered who played that role for him. Maybe not now — maybe there comes a time when you're no longer in the market for heroes. But what about back when he was looking? What about when he felt the need for someone to look up to?

"My heroes are and were my parents," he said. "I can't see having anyone else as my heroes. Because of the situation I'm in, I've seen a lot of what people expect in heroes. People expect their heroes to be flawless, never to make mistakes, to be happy all the time. And no one can do that. No one never makes mistakes, and no one always does everything right, and I can tell you for sure that no one is happy all the time."

Most people, however, when they think of heroes think of larger-than-life figures. Your parents, no matter how much you respect them, are the people around the house. They don't loom as imposingly to you as

After fourteen years in the NBA, Michael Jordan retired. Many people consider him the greatest basketball player ever; some might even say he's the most famous living human being in the world. Michael's achievements, on and off the court, are fine examples of my father's nine values working in harmony.

does a distant idol on a movie screen or a rock concert stage. Or a basketball court.

"You can't really depend on those other people for guidance, though, or for setting an example you see every day," Jordan said. "I can admire someone's talent and respect that person, but I leave it at that. I don't think I could ever pattern my life after another person. Because each person can only be himself — there's only one of each person. As hard as you try, you're always going to be that one person."

"What was it about your parents that made them heroic to you?" I said.

"It wasn't that the rest of the world would necessarily think that they were heroic," he said. "But they were the adults I saw constantly, and I admired what I saw. I don't know how many children can say that. My father was and is a very smart man. He was homemade smart — he never went to college. So he made himself smart in a sense, he learned about things all by himself, and that taught me something about making yourself better. My mother always had a job when I was growing up, and when I saw her leaving the house to go to work it made me know there was something good about the discipline of accepting what your job is and then fulfilling your responsibilities to that job. My father was very funny around the house, and I liked to watch his mind work; my mother was very focused, and by watching her I learned that you have to be serious about what you want out of life."

"This life you're going through, now," I said. "Has it had the effect of souring you on the whole idea of heroes?"

"I'm not sure whether anyone, if he's telling the truth to himself in the middle of the night, is a hero to himself," Jordan said. "You're not a hero when you look at yourself. You just try to do the best that you can. And you don't learn that from a sports star or a TV star. If you're lucky, you grow up in a house where you can learn what kind of person you should be from your parents. And on that count, I was very lucky. It may have been the luckiest thing that ever happened to me."

Oprah Winfrey

as told to Brian Lanker

ONE OF THE GREATEST ASSETS I have is good timing. I had the good timing to be born in 1954, the year of *Brown v. Board of Education*. I'm a product of desegregation. That has enabled me to become as successful as I have, financially, emotionally, and spiritually.

I am grateful and blessed because those women whose names made the history books, and a lot who did not, are all bridges that I've crossed over to get to this side. I stand here on solid ground because of them. . . . Recognizing that I am a part of that history is what allows me to soar.

I was raised to believe that excellence is the best deterrent to racism or sexism. And that's how I operate my life.

It never occurred to me that I was less than anybody else, because I was always ahead of everybody else. . . .

. . . One of my main goals on the planet is to encourage people to empower themselves. I do that

As Oprah Winfrey continues to expand her multimedia conglomerate, she never loses sight of her goal: to make a difference in other people's lives.

through my work on television and my work socially with organizations and my work in my relationships. . . .

For a lot of people, I recognize that I carry their dreams. When they see me, they see themselves. And it's all right for me to make a million dollars because they can conceive of themselves making a million. . . .

I don't fit other people's expectations. . . .

. . . I'm not controlled by the material things. I'm not defined by them at all. The only difference between being famous and not is that people know your name. It's very easy to get lazy when you get rich and forget where you came from. So the challenge is to never forget. You're here to do something, not just lay back and sit poolside. The challenge is to use this power, use this fame to help other people and do it in ways that are inspiring . . . And that's why I've formed my own company. Rather that complain about television and get upset about it and angry, I've decided I'd start changing it myself.

COURAGE DETERMINATION

TEAMWORK PERSISTENCE

INTEGRITY CITIZENSHIP

JUSTICE COMMITMENT

EXCELLENCE **EPILOGUE**

DETERMINATION TEAMWORK

PERSISTENCE INTEGRITY

CITIZENSHIP JUSTICE

COMMITMENT EXCELLENCE

EXCELLENCE COURAGE

DETERMINATION TEAMWORK

PERSISTENCE INTEGRITY

Jackie's Nine

WE'VE COME TO THE END OF *JACKIE'S NINE* and isn't it fitting that we concluded with the value excellence? I intentionally structured the book so that it would build to this point.

Excellence is the culmination of putting your best effort into whatever you're trying to do. It is believing in yourself, staying focused and expecting the best. Excellence is achieved when Jackie's nine values work in concert: you can't have courage without integrity; commitment demands teamwork and depends upon determination; persistance and citizenship lead to justice.

My father and mother were my best heroes. They taught me about these nine values, they lived these nine values. From them, I learned how to face life's obstacles and still focus on excellence. I've made mistakes along the way but I have few regrets.

Each day, we all face some barrier, but it's how we approach that barrier that really matters. It begins with loving ourselves and striving toward excellence in everything we do. It continues with self-confidence that's gained from each small victory; and the strength that is gathered with each challenge.

My dad taught me that a life is not important except for the impact it has on other lives — I've adopted his philosophy.

After opening day 1997, I was convinced that it was time for me to link directly to my dad's baseball legacy. Breaking Barriers became that link. We use it to empower students with strategies to help them face obstacles in their lives.

Working with the Office of the Commissioner of Major League Baseball, allows me to get out into communities from Seattle to Kalamazoo. I was thrilled when Derek Jeter asked me to join in his Turn 2 Foundation's effort to reach kids in Michigan.

Baseball stars like Eric Karos, Brian Hunter, Alex Rodriquez, Tony Gwynn and Mike Piazza are among the numerous Major Leaguers who have visited schools all over the U.S. and Canada as part of Major League Baseball's Breaking Barriers program.

A Temple of God

by Reverend Jesse L. Jackson

Jack Roosevelt ("Jackie") Robinson, 1919–1972

The Reverend Jesse L. Jackson, Baptist minister, national political figure, freedom fighter, author, and dear friend, delivered this stirring eulogy at my father's funeral at Riverside Church in New York City on October 29, 1972. There were a number of speakers that day but it was especially important to my family that Jesse Jackson give the eulogy because he represented the future. At the time, I was too numb to absorb the full text of his message. Two days later, I heard it repeated on an NPR radio station and I called Reverend Jackson up to thank him. His words infused me with faith and the courage to see beyond the pain of the moment.

◆ ◆ ◆

JACKIE'S BODY WAS A TEMPLE of God, an instrument of peace that had no commitment to the idle gods of fame and materialism and empty awards and cheap trophies.

Jackie, as a figure in history, was a rock in the water, hitting concentric circles and ripples of new possibility. Jackie, as a copartner with God, was a balm in Gilead, in America, in Ebbets Field.

When Jackie took the field, something within us reminded us of our birthright to be free. And somebody without reminded us that it could be attained. There was strength and pride and power when the big rock hit the water and concentric circles came forth and the ripple of new possibility spread throughout this nation.

He didn't integrate baseball for himself. He infiltrated baseball for all of us, seeking and looking for more oxygen for black survival, and looking for new possibility.

His feet on the baseball diamond made it more than a sport, a narrative of achievement more than a game. For many of us, it was a gift, of new expectations, on that dash.

He helped us to ascend from misery to hope, on the muscles of his arms, and the meaning of his life. With Rachel, he made a covenant, where he realized that to live is to suffer, but to survive is to find meaning in that suffering. Today we can raise our hands and say Hallelujah!

In his last dash, Jackie stole home. Pain, misery, and travail have lost. Jackie is saved. His enemies can leave him alone. His body will rest, but his spirit and his mind and his impact are perpetual and as affixed to human progress as are the stars in the heavens, the shine in the sun and the glow in the moon. This mind, this mission, could not be held down by a grave.

No grave can hold this body down. It belongs to the ages, and all of us are better off because the temple of God, the man with convictions, the man with a mission, passed this way.

PERMISSIONS

Pages 9-14: "In the Shadow of Your Wings," by Sharon Robinson. From *Stealing Home: An Intimate Portrait of Jackie Robinson* by Sharon Robinson. Reprinted by permission of HarperCollins Publishers. Copyright (©) 1996 by Sharon Robinson.

Pages 15-19: "The Meeting," by Jules Tygiel. From *Baseball's Great Experiment: Jackie Robinson and His Legacy*, 2nd Edition by Jules Tygiel, Copyright (©) 1997 by Jules Tygiel. Used by permission of Oxford University Press, Inc.

Pages 20-25: "She Walked Alone," by Daisy Bates. From *The Long Shadow of Little Rock* by Daisy Bates. Reprinted by permission of the University of Arkansas Press. Copyright (©) 1986 by Daisy Bates.

Pages 29-32: "The Capping Ceremony,"by Sharon Robinson. From *Stealing Home: An Intimate Portrait of Jackie Robinson* by Sharon Robinson. Reprinted by permission of HarperCollins Publishers. Copyright (©) 1996 by Sharon Robinson.

Pages 33-37: "Breaking the Color Barrier," by Jackie Robinson. From *I Never Had it Made* by Jackie Robinson, an autobiography as told to Alfred Duckett. Reprinted by permission of the Robinson Family.

Pages 38-41: "Still Me" by Christopher Reeve. From *Still Me* by Christopher Reeve. Copyright (©) 1998 Cambria Productions, Inc. Reprinted by permission of Random House, Inc.

Pages 53-57: "The Colonel from Old Kaintuck," by Carl Rowan. From *Wait Til Next Year* by Carl Rowan and Jackie Robinson. Copyright (©) 1960 by Carl T. Rowan and Jack R. Robinson. Copyright renewed 1998 by Carl T. Rowan and Rachel Robinson. Reprinted by permission of Random House, Inc.

Pages 58-62: "Together Now! Push!" Copyright (©) 2000 by David Robinson.

Pages 65-67: "Getting Beyond Average" by Sharon Robinson. From *Stealing Home: An Intimate Portrait of Jackie Robinson* by Sharon Robinson. Reprinted by permission of HarperCollins Publishers. Copyright (©) 1996 by Sharon Robinson.

Pages 68-70: "Wait Til Next Year," by Jackie Robinson. From *I Never Had it Made* by Jackie Robinson, an autobiography as told to Alfred Duckett. Reprinted by permission of the Robinson Family.

Pages 71-78 "The Great One," by Bruce Markson. From *Roberto Clemente: The Great One* by Bruce Markson. Reprinted by permission of Sports Publishing Inc. Copyright (©)1998 Bruce Markson.

Pages 81-83: "Love and War" by Sharon Robinson. From *Stealing Home: An Intimate Portrait of Jackie Robinson* by Sharon Robinson. Reprinted by permission of HarperCollins Publishers. Copyright (©) 1996 by Sharon Robinson.

Pages 84-89: "The Lion at Dusk" by Roger Kahn. From *The Boys of Summer* by Roger Kahn. Reprinted by permission of the author.

PHOTO CREDITS

ABOUT THE AUTHOR

Sharon Robinson is Jackie Robinson's daughter and the Director of Educational Programming for Major League Baseball. She is the author of a family biography, Stealing Home, *and is the creator of* Breaking Barriers, *an in-school program of Major League Baseball, the Major League Baseball Players Asscociation, and Scholastic.*

Prior to joining Major League Baseball, Ms. Robinson had a 20-year career as a nurse-midwife and educator. She has taught at Yale, Columbia, Howard, and Georgetown universities. She has also served as director of the PUSH for Excellence Program and as a fund-raiser for the United Negro College Fund and A Better Chance.

Ms. Robinson is the mother of Jesse Simms. She lives in New York City.